Face to Face with Transforming Fear into Love

Krishnananda Trobe, MD
With
Amana Trobe

(A New and Revised Edition 2009)

Perfect
ublishers Ltd

i

Copyright © Krishnananda Trobe, MD, Amana Trobe

ISBN 978-1-905399-40-6

Cover Design
Anugito, Artline Graphics, Sedona, Arizona
artline@northlink.com

Cover Artwork
Michael Colpitts, Sedona, Arizona www.artfulceramics.com

Edited by Jan Andersen
http://www.creativecopywriter.org

PERFECT PUBLISHERS LTD
23 Maitland Avenue
Cambridge
CB4 1TA
England
http://www.perfectpublishers.co.uk

About the Authors

For information about seminars, individual and couples' work, as well as other books and cds by Krishnananda and Amana, go to: www.learningloveinstitute.com or email to: info@learningloveinstitute.com.

Table of Contents

Introduction

There is a common misconception about fear that it is something negative, something to be avoided or to be overcome. That, at least, was my perspective for many years. But I learned over time that by facing my fears, I began a profound journey which took me deep inside. This book describes that journey, a healing process, based on learning to deal with our fears in a loving and compassionate way. It is based on my own inner process and also on the material which my partner, Amana, and I use in the seminars we lead around the world. We have discovered that much of what holds us back from living a fulfilling life is fear that we have not explored and integrated. The more we are able to accept and work through our fears, the more we are able to live our life in the fullest and most rewarding way possible. But on an even deeper level, facing and embracing our fears is a doorway to the divine, to a profound connection to existence. It opens us to our vulnerability.

As I consider the major events of my life, it seems they have revolved around dealing with my fears one way or another; the fears of loss, of punishment, of criticism and judgment, of rejection, loneliness and abandonment, fears of survival, of exposure and humiliation, of success or failure, of intimacy, of confrontation and anger or of losing control. And each time that I have been able to move through a significant fear and relax with it, it has marked a new stage of self-discovery and depth.

A friend and mentor of mine used to say that we can choose to live in the jungle or in the garden. In the jungle, we are taken over and live by the values of struggle, competition, success or failure, image and performance, where we see people living in a hierarchy based on success, attractiveness and power and there is a predominant feeling of scarcity and fear. In the jungle, we are taught to push through fear and this attitude forces us to either compensate for our vulnerability and fear or collapse.

In the garden, the world is a place where there is space for everyone to express himself or herself in his or her own way. In the garden, there is acceptance for whatever space we find ourselves in. It is a world in which the highest values are acceptance of what is, and supporting each other to learn to love ourselves, to discover and develop our own value and gifts without comparison. It is a world of learning to see others not as threats, but as resources. Perhaps, in our heart, we would prefer to live in the garden, but our minds and behavior may remain lodged in the jungle. It takes a little shift of consciousness to change our point of view.

Many of us, perhaps most of us, have been raised in a jungle atmosphere; in an atmosphere of pressure, tension and comparison, where we were judged and evaluated based on performance and appearance rather than being. This kind of conditioning is deeply rooted in the societies in which we grew up and gets transmitted unknowingly and automatically from one generation to the next. When we have been raised in this kind of environment, we end up carrying a tremendous amount of fear and shame in our minds and bodies. Our sense of self becomes damaged and we lose an innate sense of trust and openness.

Living in "jungle" consciousness is painful. When I remind myself of some of the things I have done (and thought) as a result of acting out of this kind of consciousness, it is hard to forgive myself. I have competed with colleagues and even wished them to fail. I have been impatient with friends, lovers and clients and sometimes even abused them with my judgments and impatience. I have been dishonest and unaccountable. I have betrayed people with my narcissism and have not been there when they needed me. I have pushed myself mercilessly, held myself to impossible standards and been hard on myself when I did not live up to my expectations. This kind of behavior comes directly from my "jungle" conditioning. It is not an excuse, but it is an explanation. Jungle conditioning builds a core of fear and from this fear, without loving awareness, we naturally act out with all kinds of destructive behaviors – to ourselves and to others.

I realized years ago, through self-work and working with others, that the root of dysfunction, sabotage and all the behaviors that I mentioned above, is fear. Fear is a core issue, perhaps *the* core issue that we all have to deal with in our lives. We can begin to understand our fear by learning what we may be afraid of, such as invasion, insensitivity, abuse, humiliation, abandonment, rejection, loneliness, isolation or annihilation. But on a deeper level, we get to know our fear by what it feels like in the body and by feeling how it drives our thoughts and our actions.

When it is denied and unacknowledged, it gets shoved into the basement of our consciousness from where it exerts a powerful and often crippling affect on our lives. Even though we may try to cover it up with all sorts of compensations and addictions, as long as it remains a hidden force, it can cause chronic anxiety, sabotage our creativity and make us rigid, suspicious and obsessed with security. Worst of all, it can destroy our efforts to find love. It is fear that keeps us living in the jungle and out of the garden. It is our fears that prevent us from recognizing our essential gifts and opening to what life has to offer.

Fear affects and often dominates all aspects of our lives; how we speak, how we work, how we eat, how we relate, how we create or how we don't do any of these because of fear. It affects how we breathe. It is an ever present factor that we attempt to ignore, overcome or push away. Somewhere along the way of my own exploration, I discovered how deep my fears were, how deep they have always been. I knew I had many fears, but my attitude was that fear was something I needed to overcome or it would limit my life and make me a coward. For as long as I can remember, I made the decision that I would not let my fears "get" to me. I used my determination and my willpower to push through them. I even remember years ago, while learning to climb rocks, that half way up a 350 foot ascent, I said out loud, "Fuck you mountain; you are not going to beat me!"

None of this was helping me become any more intimate with myself. I was running from my fears. And this avoidance was splitting me from my own vulnerability and my depth. That split showed itself in my relationships. My lovers were carrying the projection of my vulnerability and I faulted them for it one way or another for being too "needy" or too fear-ridden. I was out of touch with myself, but I believed that if I ever stopped to investigate my fears, they would simply take over. In short, I developed a lifestyle that was built on a creative compensation for all of my fears. I worked hard in school, I kept myself busy doing things, I challenged myself with risky activities and I avoided intimacy. I pushed and pushed, I rushed from one thing to another, I accomplished, I pleased and I looked for approval and recognition, all to avoid feeling the fears and emptiness inside.

Of course, I did not know that I was on a treadmill to avoid fear. I just thought that living this way was how life was. I did not recognize another way of living until much later. As long as I was trapped in all this fear compensation, I could not see that it was a way of living that was deeply engraved in Western culture, so deeply imbedded in the culture that it seemed almost unthinkable to break out of it. It took me many years of soul searching before I discovered how deeply trapped I was, that I was in an unconscious "coping trance", the trance of running away from fear all the time to cover up a little boy inside who was terrified of failure and of rejection. Even my habitual spacing out and withdrawing was a cover for fear; the fears of a child who was in shock much of the time.

When fear is unrecognized and undealt with, it causes lovers to fight, become co-dependent and, eventually, to part. It cripples our ability to have intimacy because our focus is not on ourselves, but on the other person, on what he or she does or doesn't do, or in all the ways he or she is not giving us what we want. Unworked through fear also cripples creativity and it destroys self-esteem. We push, judge and criticize ourselves and others, we compare ourselves endlessly, try to improve our image and lose ourselves in the search for approval, respect and recognition. Furthermore, unrecognized and undealt with fear causes us to act out unconsciously and that is painful and destructive to ourselves and to those we come close to. Unprocessed fear also causes separation by allowing us to cling to the belief that the world is an unloving and uncaring place. Unless we heal this mistrust, it leaves us feeling separate and separation prevents us from receiving love.

Now, I know that there is another way to approach fear. I have learned and am still learning about trauma and the affects it has on one's nervous system. I am taking the time to track the fear sensations in the body when they get provoked and notice how fear affects my thoughts and behavior. In this book, I present a method for healing and for moving from "jungle" to "garden" consciousness which Amana and I use in our work and one which I continually use in my own life. This method involves learning to accept and understand our fear both in the ways it shows itself in our life today and also how it developed as a result of childhood experiences. It includes developing the ability to actually feel how fear presents itself in the body and learning to notice how and when our thinking process is driven by fear.

The method we teach not only involves learning to "feel" fear; it also involves learning how to develop energy in the body so that we can retrieve the life energy that we lost as a result of trauma and negative conditioning. This includes learning to build strength and confidence in the body. Building energy and strength also includes incorporating a quality of risk into our life, which helps to build confidence, self-trust and self-esteem. The areas of risk are different for each of us. Part of our healing is learning where to take risks at any particular moment in our life. They also have to be such that they challenge our fears but don't overwhelm us with feelings of failure and helplessness.

In this book, I reveal, at times, painful experiences from my own childhood, not to cast blame on my parents or anyone else, but simply to share some of my own wounding. As I have written this book, I have actually felt deep gratitude for the gifts and inspiration that I received from my parents. But like all parents, the unconsciousness from their own unhealed wounds left

xi

wounds which I needed to open and heal. I share my own experiences also to point out the origin of the negative conditioning that all of us received. My process has been a journey; first out of the denial that I had a "good" childhood, then into the feelings of anger and grief for the pain that I went through and finally how I have used all of these experiences to learn how to live more and more in "garden" consciousness. Fear and pain are great teachers if we can learn how to deal with them.

I also share, in small ways throughout the book, the inspiration that I have received from my spiritual master who has taught me, among other things, the gift of meditation and of celebrating life. The term, "the great affair" has been used in the Zen tradition to describe the process of learning to trust a spiritual master as a way of learning to trust in life. I can recognize that this has been a large part of my journey through my own fears. Along the way, I also provide examples from our work with people, exercises and guided meditations to help you integrate what I am giving. The issues that I deal with are issues that affect all of us deeply and even though we all have individual differences, we also share common themes. And perhaps deep down, we are all looking for the same thing; an ability to accept and love ourselves and to share that love with another person.

When I started my training in psychiatry, on one of the first days at the hospital, I noticed a woman crawling on the floor of the ward. I knew her name from her chart and went up to her and asked, "Mary, what are you doing?" She looked up at me and quite sincerely and honestly answered, "I'm doing the best I can." I had nothing else to say, but Mary taught me a great lesson that day.

Chapter 1

A Model for Healing – An Overview

"The center of our life, your being, is your connection with the cosmos. From this door, you can enter into the cosmos and become one with existence. But even to be at the center... you will find great splendor and mystery. This has been called the Buddha, the awakened one. This moment you are all Buddhas. You may forget, but that does not matter. You will remember again."

Osho Zen, The Mystery and Poetry of the Beyond

In this chapter, I present a model, an energy picture of our being as most of us regularly experience it. This model is also a description of our wounding and a map of our recovery. We use this model in our work as an anchor for the journey of returning to "garden" consciousness. The journey we are on is basically a return to a space inside that we have lost and this model describes that process. In presenting this model, I include some psychological and spiritual material in a way that is as simple and straightforward as possible.

Imagine that you are standing in the center of a large circle divided into three rings. There is an outer ring, a middle ring and a center, an inner core. These rings radiate out from you. The outermost ring, we call the layer of protection. The second ring is the layer of our wounded vulnerability, a place where we experience fear and shame. Finally, the center is the core of being, the seat of our essence, a space in which we are in a flow with existence. In the center, we are in a deep relaxation with life, appreciating our gifts and our uniqueness and no longer feeling the need to struggle. Our journey is not only to rediscover our essential nature, but also to develop deep compassion and understanding for our wounding and our protection as well. Let's explore each of these layers in more detail.

1

The Center – Our Essence and Core of Being

When we are in the center, we feel at *one with ourselves, with life and with existence*. We feel love, trust, aliveness, joy, innocence, excitement, stillness and relaxation. This space is quite familiar in spiritual traditions that teach the practice of meditation as a path of transformation. It is a space of acceptance of life, compassion, let go, trust and non-efforting. When we are in the center, our life energy and vitality flows naturally out from this inner space in a spontaneous way whether it is in creativity, sexuality, deep emotions, assertion, dance, playfulness, sports or any way in which energy can move.

We are born in the center. We arrive in this world in a state of pure innocence and trust, naturally loving and alive. We have no protection because we have not yet experienced a need to build one. We are naked and utterly vulnerable. We have no identity, name or address; we just are. But we lose this pristine innocence and trust through traumas of one kind or another and that causes the other two layers to form. It is not unfortunate that we lose this state, because it presents us the challenge of replacing unconscious innocence and trust with conscious innocence and trust. It is only sad when we cannot find it again.

Most of us have moments in which we re-experience the center one way or another. Perhaps in meditation practice, we may feel moments of oneness, stillness and deep relaxation. Perhaps in making love, we may experience a deep melting and oneness, not only with the person we are loving, but with life itself. We can feel this space of aliveness, centeredness and flow while in creativity, martial arts, dance, athletics (what trained athletes call "the zone"), or even during a period of intense grief when we have gone deeply inside. But usually, these are brief glimpses. The process of returning to the center to the point where it really becomes home and a familiar abode involves a process of learning about the other two layers and learning how to integrate them in our life.

The Middle Layer – Our Wounded Vulnerability

As a child, most of us received some kind of trauma, whether it is rejection, repression of our vital life energies, insensitivity, lack of warmth, tension or abuse, comparison, pressure, criticism or judgment. Perhaps the greatest insult of all is that rather than being supported to become the person we are, we are conditioned to become the person that others (parents, teachers, society as a whole) expect and want of us. With these insults, our innocence, aliveness, lovingness and trust begins to fold in on itself. Innocence turns to suspicion, trust turns to mistrust, spontaneity turns to collapse and self-doubt, aliveness can turn to depression and lack of energy, natural assertion turns to either belligerence or inability to defend ourselves, enthusiasm turns to worry, flow turns to push. The list goes on. We become wounded.

This wounding happens at different times in our life, as early as the womb or continuing in our life of today. It happens to each of us in different ways and in different doses. And naturally, we are each affected differently, but it is important to recognize that it happens to all of us. Very few of us (I have met only one person in my life for whom this process did not happen) have the inner resources as a child to defend ourselves effectively against abuse, insensitivity and negative conditioning and maintain a strong and centered sense of self.

Vulnerability in its natural state is soft, receptive, expansive and blissful. But without inner and outer trust, *vulnerability becomes mixed with fear, loneliness and shame,* as it is after our wounding. This middle layer has become a place of fear, isolation and shame. Throughout the ages, society and religion have attempted quite successfully to stamp the individual into conformity, repressing the person's wildness, sexuality and authenticity. This is because individuality is too threatening and arouses too much fear in those who wield power over the child. Fear and guilt are used universally to repress the child's vital energies and cause us to forget our true selves. Our parents, teachers and religious figures (depending on our individual story) were unknowing

3

instruments of this repression. How could they do otherwise? They too were helpless instruments of this repression.

Unless we behaved and became as we were expected and pressured to behave and become, we faced being cut of from our source of love and approval. As a child, unless we comply, we face punishment, abuse, isolation, rejection and even feelings of annihilation. Our caretakers and teachers, believing that they were acting in our best interests, enforce cultural and societal repressive values on us. So, in our innocent and receptive state as a child, we succumbed, giving up our spontaneous aliveness and wildness in exchange for love and approval. Each of us fared differently under this direct assault and found different ways to cope. (Our coping strategies fall into the layer of protection, the third and outer layer.)

But whatever our survival strategy may have been, our vulnerability is now covered with a cloak of shame and shock. And with this shame and shock are also deep feelings of betrayal, hurt, rage, helplessness and despair. This is the hurt and rage of being abused, neglected, unaccepted, unseen, not listened to, unappreciated, misunderstood; of being pressured to perform and conform and being forced to repress our sexuality and aliveness. This rage and hurt is held in the middle layer right under the shame and shock. When we explore the middle layer, most of us will first encounter the shock and shame. But with deeper exploration, we also meet profound feelings of rage, emptiness, sadness, loneliness and a hollow sense of self.

The Third Layer – The Layer of Protection

The story is not yet over. In the process of our development, we cover both the middle layer of woundedness and our essential core with a third layer, the layer of protection. We naturally built this layer to protect our wounded vulnerability. It is a shield that we created to block out painful energies from hurting us and it is the way in which we were able to take some control over our often chaotic life. Our protection tries to keep us from feeling more pain and fear. We do this in many ways; by *constricting our life energy* and experience to keep us safe, by *distracting ourselves with addictions* whether they are substances or behaviors, by fighting, pleasing, withdrawing, mentalizing, seducing, keeping busy and so on. Some of us simply blended our identity and behavior into what was wanted of us and managed to do reasonably well with our assigned tasks *(compliance)*. Others of us rebelled, but perhaps still carry feelings of deep alienation, anger and disconnection *(rebellion)*. Some of us could not meet the expectations we were given or withstand the pressure and collapsed or pulled away *(withdrawal)*. I notice that while I fit mostly into the "complier", I have a lot of the "rebel" and "withdrawer" as well.

One of the major ways that we protect our vulnerability is by adopting a *role* and a *self-image*. We form all kinds of roles to hide behind; being powerful, being a victim, being sexy, a good caretaker, being "the best" or "the worst", being funny, spiritual, charming or athletic. We can hide behind anything that fortifies our ego. I have used being a Harvard graduate, a hippy, a rebel, a doctor, a nice guy, a spiritual seeker, a psychiatrist, a therapist, a tennis player. It is unthinkable to imagine relating without a mask - a self-image that we can depend on. Without it, we feel extremely vulnerable. We lose the shelter for our fears and shame and they become exposed.

I recently went to a seminar as a participant as part of a three-year training I was doing. Normally in such a setting, I am the group leader. I have a comfortable role that I can hide behind and it shields me from my vulnerability. But this role was not available to me in this case. Furthermore, I was a newcomer to the group because I transferred from another part of the country where I had begun the training and I felt like an outsider. On the second day, I was already noticing my insecurity coming up and I retreated more and more inside. I felt so awkward and unsure of myself, I was even afraid to ask someone to have lunch with me. By the third day, I was also beginning to touch deep feelings of shock and helplessness. I recognized that all of these feelings were part of the reason I was there, but it still did not make them any more comfortable to feel. By the third day, the leader went around the

5

room asking people if they had anything to share. I wanted to stay hidden, but I soon realized that he was planning to call on all of us. By the time, he came to me, I was so nervous I could hardly speak. But he helped me expose my fears and validated the shock state I was in and I began to feel safe and integrated with myself and the group.

The layer of protection is not a negative space. It is our unconsciousness about it that can make it negative. As children, we needed to find a way to protect ourselves and most of us did by building our own unique style of protection. Without it, we may not have survived with our sanity, but unfortunately, we have become so identified and attached to our protection, that we live in it quite unconsciously. And because it has become so habitual and unconscious, it is not something which we can take on and off at will. We formed these protections so early and so unknowingly that they have become deeply habitual. Now, we keep energies out, indiscriminately leaving us isolated and unnourished. We constrict our life to limit fear and our life energy and joy suffers. Our protective shield keeps our life energy locked inside, cutting us off from our feelings and from the free flow of our creative and vital energies. Then we build a rigid belief system to defend our defenses.

Protection Invites Protection

The conflicts we have with others occur most of the time when two protective layers clash. Often, we get rejected because are approaching the other person with protection rather than vulnerability, but we are not aware of it. We may come with the idea that we are open and available, but in reality, we are in our protection, waiting for the other person to open so that we can feel safe. Then we may get indignant when we don't get back what we want.

Too often, we get lost in interacting with each other from the layer of protection and we don't know the doorway out of this situation. We try to resolve problems, but all that is often needed is to realize what state of consciousness we are in. As long as we are attempting to change or affect the other person in some way, we are in our protection. This may include having expectations, wanting to hurt the other person, trying to control, judge, manipulate or change others. Every time we are coming from this energy, we are attacking. And attack meets either counterattack or withdrawal.

It is not easy to look at our protections. We tend to be defensive about them. Without inner work, we believe that our protection is our survival and we cannot imagine another reality. But the price of unworked with protection is high. Our life and energy is constricted. Our heart stays closed and we feel isolated because protection pushes others away. We expect others and the world to make things feel safe for us and when *it doesn't happen the way we want, we either go into a state of resignation or anger.* When confronted with imagined or real threat, pressure, criticism or judgment, we react automatically, habitually and unconsciously. When we have not explored our layer of wounded vulnerability, we stay in our layer of protection. We are usually disconnected and we have difficulty feeling ourselves. *Our emotional nature is either shut down or hysterical.* We are afraid to open because we don't want to feel pain or fear.

The Road Back Home

It is healing to approach our woundedness and our protection with gentle, loving awareness. A profound inner change begins to happen once we learn to relate to our defenses without judgment and without wanting them to disappear or change. Instead, we can simply become aware *when* they arise, *how* they feel and *why* we are in a state of protection. Then they slowly begin to dissolve. In a similar way, if we can bring our shame and fear out of denial, face it directly and take the time to feel it, our core begins to shine through. And when we explore, validate and feel the shame and shock in the middle layer, diving deeply into these feelings when they arise, we start to reconnect with our beauty, power, uniqueness and preciousness. As we become less weighted down with guilt and fear of retribution, rejection and disapproval, we can take bigger risk asserting our vital energy.

7

The essence of healing, as I will explore extensively in this book, is simply to allow ourselves to be totally present to what comes up in each moment and relate to it as energy, either moving or stuck in the body.

When we notice that we are the outer layer - in our protection - we allow ourselves with gentleness and understanding to be present to this as an energy phenomenon. When we are in the middle layer - in our woundedness - we do the same. We allow ourselves to feel it as energy. Our wounding is not a problem. Problems arise when we are not in touch with it and when we lack the tools and support to work through it. Shame, fear and shock are not a curse; they are rites of passage. When we have not worked with this part of us, we tend to be disconnected from our heart. Experiencing the fear and pain in our middle layer softens us. It rounds our energy and deepens our soul. It opens a wide inner space where there is an understanding that fear and pain are feelings that everyone has and are an integral part of life. Accepting rather than fighting with fear and pain, discomfort, disappointment and even tragedy opens a door to our essential nature.

Becoming More Intimate with Ourselves

Using this map as a guide, we can begin to see and feel where our consciousness is coming from at any given moment of time. Depending on circumstances in our daily life, we can find ourselves in protection, in shame and fear, or in essence. The key is learning to watch these different states with a bit of distance. This is what, in meditation practice, is called "witnessing", simply watching what arises in consciousness from moment to moment without judgment or wanting to change anything. Life events trigger a reaction inside. Perhaps they bring us into protection, perhaps they bring up shame and fear or perhaps they bring up joy, love, excitement or bliss. As a witness, we can allow ourselves to become aware of the trigger, feel the sensations in the body and notice the thoughts that come up. The

8

witnessing allows us to become more intimate with our inner world.

With this overview in mind, we can plunge into the journey of healing.

******

Part 1

The Roots of Fear and Insecurity

Chapter 2

Recognizing and Accepting Our Fear –
Making Friends with Our Panicked Child Inside

Fear is the root of dysfunction, prejudice, protection, violence and collapse. It is behind our co-dependency, conflicts in relationship, avoidance of intimacy, self-sabotage, strategies of control, judgmentalness and perfectionism. It is behind our avoidance of the new, of new people, different ways of thinking and different ways of living. It can also be the root cause of many physical ailments, such as asthma, panic attacks, skin eruptions, digestive problems, chronic pain and chronic fatigue, to name a few. Fear often prevents us from being present and therefore cripples our aliveness and vitality. When fear rules our mind, we cannot experience and enjoy life. Fear in itself is not the problem. It is unacknowledged, unfelt and unaccepted fear that creates problems in our life. Therefore, our journey of recovery begins by exploring fear.

Using the Metaphor of the Panicked Inner Child

I would like to take a moment now to explore with you the space that I will deal with in this chapter. Imagine that you are looking at a frightened child. This child might be someone that you know, or perhaps it is just a child. Perhaps this child is very young, perhaps he or she is a toddler, or perhaps older. Take a moment to allow yourself to feel the fear of this child. Something is causing this child to be afraid, but you don't know what it is and perhaps he doesn't know what it is either. He is not sure that it is safe to show himself. Perhaps he senses a threat or perhaps he shrinks from some pressure or expectations. It doesn't matter. If you look closely, you might even see that in the eyes of this child there is mistrust, confusion and panic. Perhaps he looks around to see what he should do. Perhaps he is restless, fidgety and perhaps his eyes are darting back and forth.

Each of us carries such a child inside of us, a space of profound fear and insecurity. Imagining this space as a child, or feeling the energy of a frightened child, is just a way to help you to connect with a space inside where we carry this deep fear and insecurity. We use the term "wounded inner child" because it is extremely helpful for several reasons:

- It helps us to tune into a part of us inside that is deeply frightened and traumatized, young, sensitive, fragile and without defenses

- It is also a part of our consciousness that is directly in touch with the trauma, as if the events that brought fear were happening right now or in the very recent past

- It also helps us to see and feel that this part of us is hidden and afraid to come out for fear of getting hurt again

- It is helpful because when we can visualize or imagine a traumatized child inside of us, which is an aspect of our inner reality, it is sometimes easier to feel the feelings in the body that come with the fear

- And finally, and perhaps most importantly, the metaphor is helpful because it helps us to take some distance from the fear and the panic. When we have a little distance from the fear, it seems to help not only to feel the fear, but also to heal it

The Panicked Child Can Run Our Life

Without our knowing it, much of our behavior and thinking is driven by this part of our consciousness that lives in fear. Our restless mind, our undercurrent of anxiety, the speed and lack of presence with which many of us live our lives, are all symptoms of this panicked child inside. The panic is directly responsible for many habitual and automatic behaviors, such as withdrawing suddenly or chronically, having tantrums or rage attacks, being moody or becoming addicted to substances or certain behaviors. Often, we can get distracted in searching for multiple causes of our difficulties in life, but when we begin to explore our fear, we can go directly to the source.

14

We have clients who have been in a love relationship for some years. They love each other but they fight a lot. Their fights are predictable; they happen when the stress involved in running their own business starts to overwhelm them. When this happens, they both get tense and testy and get on each other's nerves. Then they escalate, feel victimized by the other, blame each other and on it goes. Many of us may be familiar with experiences like this one. The root is simple; it is fear. And when they fight, it is fear facing fear.

I had to go through what seems like mountains of denial and protection to begin to feel and see through the eyes of my panicked child. When I finally began to get down there, I also could see why I had covered it up for so long. It was not easy to admit to myself that I was carrying so much fear inside. It didn't fit with the image I had of myself. It has been helpful to me to understand some of the origins this fear and I have spent a lot of time doing that, but I think that I will never know where it all comes from. Perhaps many of us won't either. But regardless, it is important to bring our fear out of denial and end our lifelong patterns of compensation and unconscious protection. Most of us also live with addictive behaviors, which are also an effort to get some distance from the fear we are holding inside.

When we start exploring our fear more closely (middle layer), we naturally also will begin to notice the ways that we have and continue to avoid it (outer layer). For years and years, I covered my fears quite effectively with a consuming program of performance, drive and obsession with being good at everything that I attempted and collecting achievements. My panicked child followed along obediently, but often he would show himself at the most "inappropriate" times such as in sports competitions, important tests, or when dating someone. In fact, he came up at most times when I felt pressure and stress. And when he showed himself, it would have the effect of causing me to freeze. Freezing is not the best thing to do when one is trying to win a tennis match, or trying to impress a woman that I wanted to go to bed with!

I remember many moments when this happened, but two significant times stand out. One was when I was taking the SAT test which, if you are planning to go to an American university, is a test that strongly determines where you will be accepted. College acceptance was a very high value in my family and my older brother was already at Harvard. Going into the test, I was extremely nervous and as the test went on, I became more and more tense. I lost the patience to read questions carefully and rather than taking the time to think them through, I just started guessing so I could move onto the next question. At one point, I was so nervous, I could hardly read the words on the page. By the end of the day, I knew that I had not done well and when I went home I felt so ashamed and depressed that I went directly to my room without telling my parents how it had gone.

The other time involved a girl. I was in my second year in college. I had a crush on a beautiful girl in one of my classes. She was so pretty that I was sure she would never consider going out with me. But I took a chance to ask her and to my astonishment, she accepted. On the way to pick her up, I was already so scared that I took some sips from a bottle of my roommate's whiskey. I was not much of drinker so just those two sips made me a little lightheaded. I managed to find her dorm and took her to a Shakespeare play that one of my friends was starring in. On the way to the theater, I was having difficulty keeping conversation going because everything that I thought of saying just didn't feel "cool" enough. I got some relief during the performance because we didn't have to talk.

Afterwards, we went to a cast party that my friend invited me to and my discomfort got worse. To ease my growing anxiety, I kept taking sips of whiskey from the alcohol table. At a certain point, I was feeling so dizzy that I told her I wanted to go outside for a little while. She suggested that she come with me and since I took that as a sign that maybe she liked me, as soon as we got outside, I kissed her. And then I vomited. I kept vomiting and was so sick that she had to take me home. Needless to say, that was not the beginning of a great romance. Now, I can laugh about it, but I wasn't laughing then.

Now I see that these kinds of situations were just the tip of the iceberg. Our fear, I feel, goes much deeper. It is intense. We have deep fears of survival, of earning enough money and of being able to support ourselves. We have fears of being sexually dysfunctional, inadequate and impotent. We have deep fears of being unloved, fears of being rejected and unwanted. We have fears of being disrespected, abused, ignored, put down, fears of confronting someone, fears of not knowing who we are. We have fears of not being able to express ourselves, of being insignificant. At a deeper level, there is always the fear of emptiness and death, which probably underlies all the other fears.

Emotional Fear and Reality Fear

When we work with fear, it is important to separate "reality" fear from "emotional" fear. Reality fear is fear that is provoked when there is some immediate threat and our nervous system becomes appropriately activated to deal with this threat, whatever it is. Emotional fear is what we bring to our present life situations from unresolved traumas from the past. It is the fear of our panicked child. Today, when we feel fear, most of the time it is not reality fear, it is emotional. Or it is reality fear strongly contaminated with emotional fear. Because of our emotional fear, it is hard for us to distinguish today when we are confronted with what feels and seems like a threat, between what is real and what is imagined. And because of our emotional fear, we also cannot deal with these situations in ways that are appropriate, centered and grounded. When we begin to explore our fears, we need to learn about our emotional fear.

The Four Big Fears of the Panicked Child

1) The fears of pressure and expectation.

2) The fears of rejection and abandonment.

3) The fears of not having space, of being misunderstood or ignored.

4) The fears of physical or energetic abuse or violation.

I have found that when I explore my fear behind opening and trusting, I always come up with one of these four. And so do the people we work with. They show up in all the major areas of our life - our sexuality, our creativity, our self-assertion, our ability to feel and how we relate with lovers, friends, acquaintances and authority figures. But rather than stay and feel them, we are accustomed to running from them in any way we can. In many respects, so many of the ways people live in the Western world is a massive compensation against feeling fear. We avoid dealing with death by surrounding ourselves with so much security and luxury that we don't have to feel how vulnerable we are to the unexpected. It's in our culture and it is transmitted to us through our parents, our teachers, our religious figures and our politicians; everyone we look up to.

However to confront our fears, we have to validate them, we have to recognize that they are there and look for where they came from. In our conditioning, there is no place for fear; we were taught to hide the fear. Our culture doesn't value being honest about fear any more than it realizes how deeply fear is indoctrinated. Anyway, how can we express what we are not even in touch with? We cover it with protection, denial and unconsciousness, hiding our vulnerability under a mask because that is what we needed to do to survive. One way or another, we managed, pretending that everything was okay. We learned how to cope. We remain hypnotized by our "coping trance", not recognizing how much fear we are covering up inside. As long as we are in this trance, we delude ourselves into believing that it is less painful to deny the fear than to allow it to surface.

Bringing the Panicked Child Out of Hiding

Normally, we do not have a loving and compassionate relationship to our fear. Instead, we relate to it by:

- Pretending that it isn't there

- Blocking it out with compensations

- Becoming a victim and blaming others, life and the weather for our fears

- Spacing out whenever fear arises

- Judging it as weak, stupid or inappropriate

- Unconsciously regressing and trying to get someone else to take care of our panicked child

- Pushing through it whenever it comes up

When our fears are covered by one of these approaches, we create an inner split. One part of us, the panicked child, goes into hiding. The other part of us, the compensated adult, does not find any value to feeling or allowing fear. But then our unrecognized and undealt with fear takes us deeper and deeper into isolation and usually we don't even know it.

Recently, at an introductory meeting for one of our workshops, we were doing a preliminary exercise to help people connect with their fears of intimacy. The suggestion was to share with the person opposite to you, assuming that this person was your lover or close friend, any fear that you have and have not expressed about coming closer to that person. After some time, one woman raised her hand and said that she could find nothing that she was afraid of. We probed a bit and she admitted that her husband rarely listens to her when she talks, but instead is usually busy reading the paper or doing something else. It turned out that as a child, no one had listened to her and actually she could not imagine that someone would take the time or the interest to listen. No one had ever loved her that much. Unsupported and invalidated, she simply lost touch with her child inside and adjusted herself to living without any intimate communication. She had covered up all of her fears with a routine survival pattern based on her early deprivation. I think this kind of phenomenon is common.

A man in one of our workshops had no notion that he was afraid. He would admit to being afraid of daring feats in nature, but could see no fear in relation to people. (Not so many years ago, it could have been me.) In the same process that we just described above in which people shared their fears with each other, he spoke very mechanically about things in his life. He had experienced so little intimacy in his life that he had no feeling for what it would be like to share closely with another. He had come to the workshop because his marriage was in trouble but had little understanding as to why. In a case like this one, which is not uncommon, we are disconnected from our own panicked child who remains in deep in hiding because it is not safe to come out and also often we are disconnected from our whole emotional world. Slowly and cautiously as the workshop continued, he became more and more in touch with the pain and anguish inside; for a child who was denied tenderness and who grew up in an environment where no one shared feelings.

Danilo?

Sometimes, people who have done much therapy and meditation also discover that they have deeper and more hidden fears inside. For me as well, as for many of my closest friends, it was not until we found ourselves separating from a loved one that we began to connect with the immensity of our inner fears. One person who has worked with us for many years and who is a highly disciplined practioner of Tibetan Buddhism began a relationship two years ago and now is discovering how desperately needy and frightened he really is. In the past, he was always the anti-dependent in relationships, wanting his freedom and complaining about the neediness of his girlfriends. Now, the tide has turned and he is faced with seeing a side of himself (the panicked child), which was hidden.

Our fear and our vulnerability are lying just under the surface of our conscious mind, always ready to be awakened. It can surface whenever we allow ourselves to come close to someone, whenever we have to take a risk and put out our creativity, or whenever we expose ourselves in any way. It comes up whenever we do something that takes us away from the familiar, the safe and the known.

Intimacy is perhaps the most common place where we have to confront our panicked child and that is why we avoid it.

If we live in our protected cocoon, never launching our energy, never taking risks into unknown and uncharted territory, we may never have to confront the tremendous fear that lies buried inside. But then we sink into boredom, frustration and depression. It takes some awareness and commitment to come out of denial, face our distractions and our addictions and get to know our panicked child.

Feeling the Fear

The easiest way to connect with our fear inside (our panicked child) is to begin to feel fear as it shows itself in the body. This simply means learning to feel the subtle and sometimes not so subtle body sensations that come with fear. Here are some of the common body sensations that come with fear:

- Feelings of constriction in the chest, in the back, in the neck, in the solar plexus, in the throat, in the belly or anywhere in the body
- Sweating in the palms or heat elsewhere in the body, cold hands or feet or generally feeling cold
- Shaking and trembling
- Rapid heartbeat
- Chronic or sudden pain such as headaches, stomach, back or muscle aches

- Restlessness or agitation as if our nervous system is speeded up from drinking too much caffeine

- Shortness of breath or tightness in the breath

- Problems with digestion, constipation, diarrhea or bloatedness

- Lack of appetite or feelings of nausea

- Feeling without support underneath you, or a falling sensation

- Attacks of panic

- A general feeling of malaise or sickness

- Insomnia or excessive tiredness

Each of us has a different way that fear shows itself in our body, but most of us will have one or several of these symptoms. When I began to observe my body more closely and more regularly, I was amazed at how prevalent my fear-related body sensations actually are. And it has helped me to know that this is fear showing itself, often for no apparent reason. Now, when I look closely, I can usually find the trigger, but fear has been in our body for so long that sometimes we cannot find an obvious and recent trigger.

The Origin of Fear

There are multiple origins for our fear and perhaps in some way, we may never know all aspects of its root. Perhaps we bring some with us from past lives. Probably we carry fear in the collective cultural heritage of our family. There is also the tremendous shock of coming out of the comfort of the womb into the world. For the first few days of my life, I nearly died of undernourishment because for some reason, I couldn't digest my mother's breast milk. My mother said that I had "diarrhea of the newborn", but I was probably saying, "Help! Let me go back to where it was so warm and safe." Add the original shock of leaving the womb in the way most of us were born and we already have sufficient reasons to be afraid. Whatever emotional, physical, or sexual abuse that we may have suffered after that just adds to the original trauma of being born. The deprivation and violation we experienced throughout childhood - the lack of approval, attention, attunement, love, respect and caring that we all experienced in one way or another - is clearly another major source of our panic. Now our child inside is always expecting, in fact dreading, more abuse and abandonment.

We had deep survival and identity needs that were not met and we lost our trust. Our needs for love and protection, acceptance, validation and approval, inspiration and direction and tender, unconditional love were not met one way or another. Now, as an adult, we still carry the primal fear of never getting the basics of what we need. The blow to our innocence and trust may have come so early that there is a basic fear that we won't survive.

Unfortunately, as a child, we weren't in a position to conclude, "Well, I can see that mom and dad have a real problem here. They can't even get along with each other and they don't seem to be too interested in me. They shouldn't have had me in the first place. It's obvious that I'm not going to get what I need here, so I think what I'll do is just check out and find myself a better situation." Most likely, any place down the block would have been as bad, or worse. With the background of emotional deprivation that most of us have, entering into our vulnerability now can bring tremendous confusion, panic, fear, self-judgment, collapse and sometimes pure terror. Why? Because our vulnerability and our innocence were betrayed.

As I develop greater understanding for the extreme vulnerability that has always been buried under all my efforting, I can appreciate more and more the reason for my panic. Now, I can see that the fear of failure, of disapproval, of feeling the constant pressure to live up to the expectations that were placed upon me by family and culture, was bringing up deep fears and as a child such fears must have been devastating. The more aware part of me no longer buys into the success program of my conditioning and recognizes that when a loved one leaves or threatens to leave, I will be fine. But my panicked child doesn't know all this. He still freaks out with the same old triggers.

And far beyond all the psychological reasons for our panic is the simple and most powerful reason of all - the realization that we are going to die. We are always facing insecurity, uncertainty and ultimately death at the hands of forces far beyond our control. No amount of insurance or protection can shield us from that fear. Deep down, we know it.

Without a foundation of acceptance and inner space, all we have is fear covered in compensation.

From the perspective of our traumatized child, vulnerability equals panic - the panic of being deserted and of being annihilated. With awareness, understanding and compassion, we can find enough trust and space to contain vulnerability, insecurity and unpredictability. Our child inside simply does not have these qualities. We have to bring these qualities to heal our panicked child. Then we can transform the vulnerability from panic to acceptance.

Accepting Our Fear

It still takes much courage and awareness for me to allow and accept my fear when it comes up. There are still the deeply seated thoughts in my mind that if I allow fear, I won't make it, that I won't be able to function, that I will be judged as weak and impotent or that there will never be an end to the fear. When it comes, even after so much time devoted to inner work, my rational mind still doesn't understand why it should be there and wants it to go away. I am afraid to feel it and afraid to share it. I still judge it and condemn myself for having these feelings. Fortunately, my deeper self knows that there is much value in allowing fear to be there.

There is always a fear that if we acknowledge our fears, they will overtake us and run our lives. But by going into them, we actually empower ourselves and build more self-respect.

EXERCISE: Exploring the Fears of the Panicked Child

Review the four basic fears:

1) Pressure and expectations.

2) Rejection and abandonment.

3) Not being given space, being ignored or misunderstood.

4) Physical or energetic abuse and invasion.

Considering each, one at a time, and ask yourself: Do you have these fears? What provokes them in your life today? What do you remember from the past that might have contributed to these fears?

How do these fears affect different aspects of your life - your sexuality, your ability to assert yourself, your creativity, your relating?

I have all of them.****** I clearly can feel
the feeling of all them on my body. It remindes
my childhood. I was always afraid of my
family. aka sister, her husband. they were
severe w/ me. a lot physical invasion.
a lot fights. I couldit say something, do something
cause it was wrong. they hited me so many times.
Said bad words. things that I never forgot. deep
in my mind,
But more than that. I feel the depth aloness,
being rejected, abandoned by life, by my dad.
my mom was so sad all the time.

25

Chapter 3

Shame –
A False Experience of Self

Recently, I was attending a seminar in Los Angeles and staying with an aunt and uncle who lived nearby. These two have always been my very favorite relatives - kind, generous, loving, fun people. Over the years, they have been a big support for me in difficult times and I have always enjoyed spending time with them. We were having dinner and their son, my cousin, had come down from Northern California to visit and join us for dinner. My cousin was sharing a story of a time, some years ago, when he had invited his parents to attend a growth seminar with him given by a teacher that he and his wife had done much inner work with. He was talking about a particularly strong moment when he and his father were sitting in the middle of the circle and he was sharing a deep pain that he felt when his father would compare him to his cousins (me and my older brother) who were living in Europe and had a reputation in the family for being "high achievers". He remembered his father saying, "I wish that you could be more like them," and felt crushed by his father's statement. In the workshop, my uncle, listened, cried and apologized for causing his son this pain.

Now, listening to the story again, my uncle said how much of a failure he felt for showing this weakness and emotion. My cousin and I both pounced on him and told him that on the contrary, it was such a sign of strength that he had the courage to listen and feel his son's pain. My cousin explained that he was a role model for the kind of father all the other people in the group wished they had had. I told him that over the years, I had always felt safe, supported and loved by him and wished that everyone could have an uncle like him. By this point in the meal, all four of us were in tears. My uncle is the sweetest person one can imagine and yet he too deeply shamed his son. Ironically, even though I was the source of the comparison for my cousin, the experience my cousin went through parallels my own. I didn't escape this kind of comparison and shaming either.

I tell this story partly because it has a happy ending. Through all the work that both my cousin and I have done with ourselves, we have reached a point where we are happy and fulfilled in our lives. But the other reason I think this story touched me is that it shows that even if we have loving and caring parents, we still get shamed. Parents shame their children by basing value and approval on achievement, image, pressure and struggle. As a child, we develop confidence, self-confidence and self-respect by having our essence mirrored back to us. This happens when as a child, we feel felt, seen, heard, supported, guided and honored for the budding individual that we are. But if, instead, we are cast into a mold of expectations and projections from others, which does not blend with our essence and our gifts, if our natural aliveness is repressed with guilt and worse, or if we feel unwanted or mistreated, we cover our essential core of self-love, enthusiasm, spontaneity and authenticity with a blanket of self-doubt, fear, insecurity and self-sabotage.

As the years go by, our disconnection from ourselves gets worse as we sink deeper and deeper into trying to be someone we are not. It's too much to expect that parents are so evolved in their own consciousness that they are able to set aside their own values, preconceptions, expectations and beliefs in order to really *see* their child. They have too much fear. And that's why 99% of children get shamed. (Perhaps saying it is 99% is being optimistic.)

My father used to tell a joke about a man who walks into a tailor shop to order a new suit. The tailor takes his measurements and asks him to return in a week. A week later, he comes back to the tailor's shop to get his new suit. But when he tries it on in front of the mirror, he notices that one arm is too short, one leg is too short and the waist is too big. When he points it out to the tailor, the tailor looking at him in front of the mirror says, "Actually, there is nothing wrong with the suit. It's just that you aren't wearing it right. Look, first you have to stretch your arm like this.

Then stretch your leg like this and puff out you belly like this. Good! Now, see, it fits just fine."

Convinced, the man limps out of the store wearing his suit. As he slowly hobbles down the street, two old ladies pass him. One says to the other, "Did you see that poor crippled man? Gee what a shame!"

"Yes," replies the other, "what a terrible shame! But did you notice that beautiful suit he was wearing?"

Little did I know that this story was about shame. Needless to say, my father didn't either. We are all that innocent and trusting man who walks into the tailor shop (our family, our culture, our schooling, our religious upbringing and so on.) We all get a suit that doesn't fit and are convinced to try and make it fit. And we have been hobbling down the street ever since, disconnected from our energy, or authenticity and our sense of self. Standing in front of the mirror, we know deep inside that the suit doesn't fit but the "tailor" had too much power and we lost confidence in that inner voice of truth. In fact, as the shame gets greater, most of us even stop hearing that inner voice.

What is Shame?

Shame is a basic feeling of inadequacy, a deep sense of being wrong, not enough or incapable. In the wonderful Australian movie, "Muriel's Wedding", which is a great movie about shame, Muriel's father is constantly telling her that she is "useless". He himself is no model of integrity and gets arrested for corruption at the end of movie. Her mother has accepted the life of a humiliated second rate woman married to a man who cheats on her behind her back, and her other siblings are equally dysfunctional. Muriel is obsessed with attempting to be popular and attractive to men like the other girls, but only succeeds at humiliating herself over and over again.

In shame, we lose touch with the ability to feel ourselves in a relaxed and accurate way and that centered inner feeling

29

becomes replaced with a feeling of emptiness. We lose touch with our vital life energy, we stop trusting ourselves and we lose the ability to feel and express ourselves. This undercurrent of shame is always there.

In my life, as long as I can remember, I have been walking a tight rope between being high functioning, high achieving and successful at what I do on the one hand and on the other, overwhelmed with shame and feelings of inadequacy. I have applied myself in school, in work and in sports, but underneath I have always had a feeling that somewhere deep inside, I just don't "make it". As a child, I wanted to just like my older brother. He was a "wunder kind" and universally respected by my whole extended family, almost mythological, it seems. When I was in tenth grade, he was awarded an honorary scholarship to Harvard because, in the words of the Dean of Admissions, he was such a "remarkable candidate", but did not qualify for financial aid. In high school, he was captain of all the teams and the editor of the school newspaper. When he graduated, he walked away with all but one of the awards. I was sitting in the audience torn between pride and feeling very small in comparison.

Naturally, all through school, I tried to be as good. I set my scopes at also being accepted to Harvard and to this day, I think that I was only accepted because my brother knew the Dean of Admissions from an article he had done on him for the Harvard Crimson, the college newspaper. He told my brother that if I was "half as good as you are, we'll take him." That's what I thought I was; "half as good." (I now know that these are the "shame voices" talking). All through college, I continued to compare myself to my brother, but toward the end of the last year, something was starting to change. At graduation, when the Dean handed me my diploma and asked me what I was planning to do, much to the dismay of my family, I said, "I don't know."

I finally had the good sense to get off the achievement train and went to California to join the counterculture. I began to experiment with new ways of living, new ways of looking at life and taking mind-altering drugs. I lived in communes in Oregon and Berkeley, California, starting practicing yoga and meditation and tried to make some sense of my life. Under the cover of being a "hippie", I was still as confused, compulsive and as dysfunctional as ever. It was going to take a lot more than living in communes and doing a few psychedelics to make a dent in my shame.

When we have shame, we may swing from feeling great about ourselves when people or life gives us recognition, approval, success or acceptance and terrible when we meet with failure, rejection, not feeling respected or appreciated. Our sense of self is dependent on outside circumstances and we believe that if we have the recognition, love, respect, approval, fame, wealth or acceptance that we long for, we will feel better and our shame will go away. Before I knew about shame, I was trapped in a never ending struggle to prove myself without any awareness that there was any other way to live nor any awareness that what I was trying to do to feel better was never going to work.

Now, I recognize that shame is quite universal. Looking into a mirror, most of us are immediately confronted with our shame. It comes out as attacking, critical, condemning judgmental voices like, "You're too old, not pretty enough, too serious, too fat, too skinny, etc." Whatever the statements, the first impression that we have of ourselves when we look into the mirror is usually one of judgment. We may try to fix what we see but we know deep down that it can't be fixed. The degree of shame differs from one person to another and we each have our own particular brand of shame. But we all have it. The point is whether we choose to heal it or continue to try and avoid it, cover it up and deny it. It was not until my forties that I began to realize how much shame I was carrying. Prior to that, I had done everything to avoid feeling insecure or showing my insecurity. My goal was to "be in my energy", succeed and win approval. Now, I realize that I prostituted myself for respect, recognition and approval. I also realized that when I was not feeling alive, vital and confident, I was in shame but now I know that it has more value to be with the shame rather than pushing it away or pushing through it.

The Causes of Shame

Each of us has our own shame story and it brings immense compassion for ourselves to discover how we have been shamed. And knowing our story does not mean to stay in blame or bitterness. We probably need to go through a period of anger and feeling betrayed when we discover the extent to which our innocence and trust was damaged, but healing shame is an essential spiritual rite of passage that we have to go through. We start with taking shame out of denial and confronting honestly and directly how it happened to us.

In the process of trying to find ourselves as a child, we are continually looking at the mirrors that the big people - parents, teachers, and older siblings - are holding up for us. Our sense of self is built of the reflections we get from these mirrors. If the mirror is positive, if we are loved and our creativity and feelings are validated and supported, we form a strong sense of self. For example, *if* our early sexual explorations were respected and supported and *if*, as we grow older, we do not pick up the message, verbally or nonverbally that sexuality is dirty, wrong or sinful and *if* our parents have a healthy relation to their own sexuality, *then* we develop a healthy relationship to our sexuality. The same is true for other aspects of our energy and feelings – anger, joy, privacy, silence, sadness, fear, or creativity. An original trust in our energy and feelings establishes a ground, an anchor in our being and a confidence with how we interact with others and the world. It gives us a confidence in ourselves, we feel connected to our body and we trust our evaluation and responses to outside reality.

But *if* the mirror reflects rejection, criticism, impossible expectations and standards we can never attain, *if* the mirror tells us our value is based on what we *do*, our sense of self shatters and we become shamed. We are so sensitive and vulnerable as a child, so needing of love and approval from our caretakers that it does not take much to discourage our learning to trust ourselves. Most of us simply do not have the resources as a child to follow our own voice rather that those of the "big people". Our survival

32

depends on adjusting ourselves to their wishes. We were handed a script based on the values of our parents and the culture they live in, which might have felt right to them but it rarely has much to do with who we are. And usually the conditioning we receive is contaminated with all the life negative and repressive attitudes, which our parents inherited from their parents and culture, who in turn received it from their parents.

The degree of shame we receive depends on how strong the negative mirror was and how early it came. Physical abuse in any form is a tremendous humiliation to a child, a profound violation of his or her boundaries and a rupture of his or her sense of self. Sexual abuse (any form of sexuality overt or covert between an adult and a child) is all of this and more. It creates a deep confusion and conflict about love and sexuality. It is not within the scope of this book to deal with abuse in any detail as this has been adequately dealt with elsewhere. (See selected references). Our shame can also come from many forms of emotional abuse; being unwanted as a child, receiving the tension or emotional instability of a parent, being criticized or humiliated, being patronized ("children are too immature to have valid opinions and feelings"), compared to another, being told what to think and what to feel, having our life energy repressed, having to take care emotionally of a parent, not receiving attention, not being listened to, or being given advice. The list goes on.

Here is a summary of some of the common causes of shame:

- Any form of emotional, physical or sexual abuse
- Experiencing abandonment and physical separations from caretakers as a child
- Receiving the life negative and repressive attitudes of our parents, teachers, religious figures and other authority figures
- Not feeling wanted or received as a child
- Being patronized, labeled and treated as a child rather than being respected as a person

33

- Being compared to someone such as a sibling, other family member, neighbor, classmate or friend

- Being judged, teased or humiliated

- Being repressed in our vital energies

- Not having our feelings, opinions or intuition validated

- Being pressured and expected to become someone or something that we are not in our nature meant to become

- Being manipulated to play an inappropriate role in the family such as a caretaker for one or both of our parents

When I first started therapy, my therapist asked me about my childhood. "I had a great childhood," I answered. "My parents were fantastic, still are. I traveled all over the world, learned lots of foreign languages and my parents supported me to get the best education possible. They really care about me." And I went into a long discourse on all the positive qualities of my father and mother. The therapist listened and simply nodded her head. Six months later, I had a very different point of view. All what I said that first day was true and still is. But what I didn't see was how deeply dysfunctional my family actually was, how troubled and superficial the relationships were and how much trauma I received from being raised in this family.

It is vital for our healing to see and feel how we gave ourselves away for love and approval and to experience the pain of this process. We still carry the negative thought forms of those who raised us. Our budding individuality and authenticity was brought down and we had no choice and no ability to resist this process. Unconsciously, we made a compromise for our survival and most of us still do. Then we forgot who we are. We conformed and became good citizens, good children, good students, good earners, good family members or we collapsed under the strain. Even if we rebelled, our rebellion is still a reaction to outside forces.

Shaming rarely comes from maliciousness; it comes from unconsciousness. Most parents lack the skills and awareness to raise a child in a nonshaming way unless they have done inner work, uncovered and felt their own shame.

For years, shaming has been an accepted form of raising children; religious repression, pressure, high expectations, even physical abuse. What will change this over time is the realization that children have an intuitive knowledge of themselves and need to be raised in such a way that they learn to discover and trust this inner knowing.

The Way Shame Affects Our Life Today

A simple way to recognize when we are in the hypnosis of shame is to notice how it shows itself in one of three areas. The first is how it feels in the body – commonly low energy, a feeling of sinking and collapse, lack of motivation, depressed and lacking enthusiasm. The second area is in our thinking – repetitive negative thoughts about ourselves, about life and about others. And the third area is in our behavior – what we call "shame behavior" – being self-destructive, aggressive toward others, reactive, impulsive, highly emotional, avoiding contact with others, excessive socializing, shopping, working, attracting those who reject us or rejecting others and so on.

When we are shame based, we deal with it either by puffing up or deflating, either by living in compensation or collapse.

The Compensated State

Many people are so well compensated that they have no clue that they are covering an ocean of inner shame. But compensated people often suffer from physical exhaustion, lack of intimacy and addiction to substances or activities that attempt to lower anxiety.

The husband of a client of ours is an extremely wealthy businessman who owns hotels and apartments all around the world. He lives the high life, flies to Chile for a weekend of helicopter skiing, has clandestine lovers and is constantly on the move, making deals with big sums of money. His wife is distraught with his secret affairs, his absence and the lack of intimacy between them, but he sees nothing wrong with his lifestyle, loves his freedom, professes his love for her and the children and is not motivated to change. Sometimes when we are functioning well in our compensations, we are only motivated to look deeper when life deals us a blow – a loss or rejection from a lover, a financial crisis and a loss of a job, or an accident, illness or death. Then our mechanisms to avoid our shame may crumble and we are faced with piecing together our fragmented self-esteem, a self-esteem that has always been fragmented because it was based on externals, not on inner knowing and strength.

Compensated people believe strongly that the world is made of "winners" and "losers". And they try to make sure that they are "winners" and stay "winners". It is much harder to recognize our shame and pain inside when we have constructed a whole lifestyle, often successfully, to avoid feeling it or dealing with it. When I look back at my years in high school and college, it seems that all I ever did was compensate for my shame. I remember so many painful moments of shaming others with my impatience and belief that only "in" people were cool. In college, one of my roommates attempted suicide because he was so unhappy. Not only could I not understand what he was going through, I even judged him for it. Compensated people shame others habitually and unconsciously. They may even believe that their shaming is justified.

We are probably aware of some of the ways that we compensate. We may use our sex appeal, charm, intelligence, ambition, speediness; anything that gives us a self-image we like and rewards us with attention and recognition. We compensate in our compulsive doing, in our addictions, in our "self-sufficiency"; anything to run away from feeling or even recognizing our profound core of shame inside. I find that often people who on the outside appear to be the most together and under control are carrying the deepest wound of shame. It is painful, but also an

36

incredible blessing when we finally see through all of our compensations and have a direct look at our shame. For me, it felt like finally coming down to earth and a powerful turn around in my world view. I came to see that believing in a world of "winners" and "losers" is a stressful and violent way to live. Coming down to my shame helped me to feel the pain others feel in their shame. It softened me and made me an easier person to be with. It made it easier for me to be with myself.

The Collapsed State

When we are shamed, something in our core starts to shrink and we lose touch with ourselves. We stop trusting our feelings, our perceptions and our energy. Instead of flowing authentically and spontaneously, we become shy, confused, held back and insecure. We are constantly under the attack of critical and condemning voices that cause us to sabotage any effort to come out of our bubble of shame. Whatever we do, it is never good enough. In relationships, we often can't feel ourselves and can't express ourselves. We don't feel attractive or desirable and every rejection or criticism just confirms what we already believe – that we are worthless. We constantly compare ourselves and always feel less than. The knots inside get tighter and tighter. In the end, our energy just collapses and can't find a way out. It may become so bad that we cannot even get out of bed. I remember when I first learned about shame, I realized that I had come to believe that shame was just how it was. I was so used to feeling humiliated that I had come to expect it and even to see myself as someone who deserves humiliation.

A collapsed shame person has often compromised for so long and so habitually, he or she simply can't imagine a state of self-respect and dignity. Our identity becomes shared-based; it is just who we are! To make matters worse, shame perpetuates more shame. When we are shame-bound, we can easily slip into the role of being a clown or a beggar. My brother used to call me, "the great source of misinformation", because in trying to impress people with my knowledge, I usually spoke about things I didn't have a clue about or, at best, got all my facts mixed up. We seek out people who make us feel inferior and then try to get his or her attention. We seek out people who are unavailable and reject us and then become a "love beggar." We find ourselves making stupid humiliating comments; the person rejects us and we feel even more shamed. It is a painful downward spiral and we perpetuate our low self esteem. I can recall countless times of humiliating myself with certain people. I hated myself for it, but I couldn't seem to control it. With certain people, I felt trapped in a cycle of humiliation and rejection. All efforts to try to be "cool" never worked.

The Shame Voices

Furthermore, shame causes us to form strong negative beliefs about ourselves and life, which can become so fixed that even if people want to convince us that we are wrong, they cannot. Some of the most common negative shame-based beliefs can be:

- "You can't trust anyone"
- "I'm not attractive"
- "I'm boring"
- "I'm too much"
- "No one could possibly love me if they knew that…"
- "Whatever I do, I will fail"
- "I need to be the best at whatever I do"
- "If I open, I will be hurt"
- "I can never get what I need because I don't deserve it"
- "I'm just too needy"
- "No one will ever understand me"

These negative beliefs become self-fulfilling. They are so ingrained in our thought structure that we live our life as if they are true. We also unconsciously broadcast our negative beliefs

38

and people to respond accordingly. If we believe that we are unlovable, it is like carrying a sign that says, "reject me". Chances are, we will get rejected. We don't see it is our shame that is affecting people. We believe that it is the truth of who we are. Our negative beliefs create an aura around us of mistrust, collapse and negativity. And so it goes on and on from year to year, from one relationship to the next.

Allowing Shame

Shame is crippling. When it rules our life, we live either in the compensated or in the collapsed state. In both cases, we cannot come home. If we don't recognize, accept and work with our shame, either we lose hope or we exhaust ourselves in trying to prove that we have value. We remain trapped in the jungle. But once we begin the process of healing, we begin to see that shame is a misconception of ourselves, a false identity, based on negative conditioning. It is a false sense of self. As we penetrate the lie and begin to re-experience ourselves in a natural and loving way, our world views changes. It is no longer about meeting impossible expectations and driving ourselves for approval. It is about relaxing and appreciating what has always been there.

When I began to learn about shame, it helped me to recognize it when it showed itself - in my energy, in my thoughts and in my behavior. I recognized "shame thoughts" and to notice how shame made my energy level drop. For instance, sometimes, I would be jogging; a shame thought would enter my mind and, immediately, I would lose the desire to keep going. I also noticed how often my behavior was shame-driven such as asking questions just to get attention or bragging about myself. I started to recognize certain triggers that predictably brought up my shame, like being with someone with whom I felt inferior or impotent. For instance, someone says something to us and we walk away feeling terrible. We visit family (a very common shame trigger) and after a little while, we start to wonder if we even have a life.

39

I was always too shame-bound to react or say anything to stand up for myself in situations where I obviously needed to set a limit. Instead I let it slide, even if there was a small echo of a voice inside saying, "Wait a minute, that didn't feel right." I was much too shocked and dissociated in such situations to respond appropriately. It was easier to minimize, think that it was my problem or excuse the other person. And then my resentment festered inside and my already low self-esteem got even worse. When around someone who intimidated me, I might become obsequious, my voice got tight in my throat and I faltered for something to say and ended up just saying something stupid or irrelevant. I recall seeing the movie, "Rambo 2" in which Sylvester Stallone spends most of the movie taking revenge for being betrayed by an officer while in the army. During the movie, I was thinking of all the people past and present in my life that I wanted to get back at and all the ways I wanted to do it.

The very first step in healing the wound of shame is to start with understanding, awareness and acceptance. It is just a shamed part of us that has a painful history, has developed a damaged sense of self and forgotten that we really are. The journey through shame brings depth and compassion to our soul. When we know and feel our own shame, we can see and feel another's as well. When we have known what we have gone through, we can tune into another person's wounding in a new way. Once, I was getting a haircut and I watched a woman who had just finished having her hair done leaving the salon. I saw from the way she looked in the mirror and walked out, that she did not have a good opinion of herself. It occurred to me how many people live in shame but they have not seen through the lie of shame.

People often ask us in our workshops, "How do I know when my shame is healed?"

Our answer is, "When your life is flowing in four main areas: You have a deepening intimacy and a nourishing sexuality. Your creativity is flowing and you can earn a decent living. You are treating your body with respect, your life energy is alive and you are no longer being self-destructive. And finally, you have found

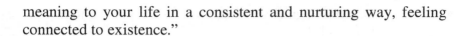

meaning to your life in a consistent and nurturing way, feeling connected to existence."

EXERCISE - Exploring Shame

The Feeling of Shame

The next time you feel low, depressed or self-critical, take a moment to feel the sensations in the body.

- What does this experience of shame actually *feel* like?
- How do you experience your energy?
- What thoughts are going through your mind?
- What is your attitude of life in this moment?

Shame Triggers

Notice specifically, what provokes you to feel bad, low and self-critical.

- Was it something that someone said?
- Was it something that you did that you feel guilty or inadequate about?
- Did you feel rejected by someone?
- Did something not happen the way you expected it to?

Your Shame Story

Looking back at your life:

- Can you remember specific times when you felt humiliated?
  do fralde, minha irmã dizendo que mati meu pai,
- Is there someone significant from your past who criticized you frequently?

  Sim, minha irmã, meu cunhado, meu irmão, meu sobrinho. "amigos" da escola.

41

- Is there someone significant from your past with whom you compared yourself?

meu irmão.

- Is there someone significant from your past who abused you?

meu cunhado.

- Did someone significant in your childhood leave you?

meu Pai

- In what ways was your vital life energy – sex, anger, joy, sadness or creativity repressed?

- What was your mother's and father's attitude toward life? Toward sex? Anger? Passion? Joy?

******

my second kiss happened when I was 13.
my sister found it out and told my mom and my dad.

I was a shame for the family.
after few weeks, my dad had a stroke and died 30 days later.

my sister blamed me for this. She said it was my fault.
I start to date online - have sex online.
Get an online life.
there I could be whatever I want and no one was blamming for it. I felt so special and loved.
People that I care found that I was lying.
I Hurted people.
feelings.
they Hurted me as well.
I'm sorry

Sex wasn't a good thing to tell about.
Anger is wrong. When you feel it, you always hurt someone.
Joy is family. Care about others.
be a good person, that's Joy.
they told me that.

42

Chapter 4

Shock –
The Frozen Form of Fear

I can't remember when I first started to learn about shock, but knowing about it changed my life. I was noticing more and more clearly that there was a deep split inside of me between one part of me that was very high functioning, intense, focused, driven and competent and another part of me that was frozen, paralyzed, spaced out and collapsed. And these two parts of me did not have a very good relationship with each other at all. My driven side was impatient and judgmental with my frightened and frozen side. My frozen side did not trust my driven side. Naturally, I projected the same split on others. If I was the driven one, I judged those I knew who were frozen as lazy or indulgent. When someone frightened me, I judged him or her as uptight, insensitive and out of touch.

Before learning about shock, I thought that something was very wrong with me when I was frozen. I thought I was basically defective; I was a coward, I was incapable of being powerful in difficult or challenging situations, I was incapable of handling any kind of pressure and I was not able to face anyone who was angry with me. Now, I know that shock is very common. Shame and its offspring, the inner judge, is crippling to our vitality and self-esteem. Shame has to do with how we think and feel about ourselves – our beliefs, our behavior and how we express ourselves. But shock hits us at such a deep level in our psyche that it affects our physiology; the way our body reacts to the outside. To be sure, shame also affects our energy, but shock seems to go to our deepest core.

Shock Symptoms

When we are in shock, often we can't think, we can't feel, we can't move and we can't talk.

43

When it arises, most of us would prefer to be able to function normally, but the shock is more powerful than our will for it not to be there. *There is nothing to do but be with it.* We would like to be centered, powerful, present, together, calm, and collected but we aren't. The more we judge ourselves about not being able to respond how we would like, the more we go into shock. I now recognize that many situations that brought me so much pain in the past, and some which still do, were situations where I was in shock but didn't know it. My performance anxiety was a symptom of shock. Choking on exams, tightening up in tennis matches, coming too fast, freezing or breaking out in a cold sweat whenever I felt pressured or expected upon, a constant underlying anxiety, a tension in my solar plexus – all symptoms of shock. In these situations, it felt to me as though my body was betraying me.

Everyone's shock symptoms are different. But there is definitely a common symptom list; confusion, spacing out, inability to remember, rapid pulse, sweating, a sense of running around in circles, paralysis, inability to speak, tightness in the chest, difficulty breathing, cold sweat, sweaty palms, or feeling an overwhelming feeling of dread or doom. Panic attacks or phobias. Sometimes, it is possible to detect the source of our shock, but often it remains a mystery.

As crippling and as devastating as shock is, it also has its value, particularly for the spiritual search. Shock is a wake-up call. When I began to recognize how often and how much of the time I was and am in shock, I also became more aware how sensitive I am. How sensitive we all are.

Shock draws attention to the incredible sensitivity of our soul; it draws attention to all the unconsciousness around us and inside of us. It pulls us out of our protected, closed and insulated world and forces us to live more consciously. It wakes us up to the pristine sensitivity of life and draws us away from the automatic, conditioned, unconscious parts of us. It awakens our vulnerability.

44

The Origins of Shock

We came into this world in an exquisitely sensitive state, with an innocence and openness that we may not be able to conceive of. That sensitivity was met with energy that often was so harsh and so abrasive that our reaction was to go into shock. To understand shock now, we have to put ourselves in the shoes of a child of pure innocence, receptivity, openness and trust, looking out at an unfamiliar and strange world. In this state of pure openness we met the world. We picked up all the vibrations in our environment. Whatever was there – perhaps our mother's tension, our father's repressed or expressed anger, or our parents yelling at each other – we felt it all and it all took us more deeply into shock. It may have been something as blatant as physical or sexual abuse. But in this early and pure state, we can sense the slightest negativity and it hits our being as a violent force.

I think I was already in shock when I was born. I think I was saying, "What am I doing here? I want go back to where it was warm and safe!" As if taking a body is not shocking enough, add to that the shock of coming out of the womb into a room with bright lights and some doctor whacking us on the buttocks. In this state of innocence, we have no ability to comprehend or incorporate this harsh energy. Each of us meets this energy differently according to what kind of resources we may have brought with us. The society we live in, no matter where it is, is not attuned to sensitivity. We learn to cover up our sensitivity as we learn to cope with life. We become hardened to the innocent child inside who went through so much to adjust. As we recover this original sensitivity, we also uncover our shock.

It is not always possible, nor is it necessary to know why we go into shock. What is most important is to validate the experience and recognize that it is not based on a deficiency in us, but on very specific and very real trauma that happened to us in the past. Some energy in the present – anger, pressure or rejection for example – is triggering a reaction inside based on a much earlier experience with a similar kind of energy.

Shock Triggers

From my experience of working with shock, I have found that there are many possible sources of shock and each one of us may have had any number of them. Today in our life, when we are confronted with one of these, with the same kind of energy that produced our original shock state, we re-experience the shock. We call these the shock triggers.

1) Overt or Covert Violence

This can be anger, hostility, judgment or condemnation. It can be any time we feel abused, used or treated unjustly, or any time we feel invaded or violated. It doesn't even have to be expressed. All we have to do is feel it and we go into shock. Most of us were exposed to some form of expressed or unexpressed anger in our childhood. It could have come from anywhere; parents, siblings, teachers or classmates and until we start to penetrate our conditioning, we are unaware of the anger that we actually encountered. It is also violent when someone tries to impose their ideas, morality and opinions on us particularly when we are in a position in which we feel that this person has some kind of power over us. As a child, many of us were told what to think, how to feel and how to behave and today, if we have had this trauma in our past, we can be easily influenced by someone who exudes confidence and strength. I recognize that this has always been a strong shock trigger for me. Because of my shame and shock, I would easily doubt my own thoughts, behavior and feelings when in the presence of someone like this.

2) Pressure and Expectations

I felt it and still do, in any kind of competitive setting. If only I had known earlier about shock, I might have saved myself much heartache for always feeling that I had "failed". Most of us have now internalized all the pressure and expectations that we received overtly or covertly in the past, so now we don't even need anyone on the outside imposing it on us. We have our own built-in pressure cooker. (And no amount of macrobiotic or

46

organic food, vitamins or studying astrology is going to take it away.) Faced with the highly competitive and patriarchal society in which most of us were raised, our child inside probably went into shock just with the anticipation of having to deal with such a world.

3) Rejection, Deep Loss or Abandonment

Many of us may not be aware or remember the sources of our abandonment wound and I will be dealing with the issue of abandonment in depth in the next chapter. Goodbyes are painful enough and when combined with a feeling of rejection, it can easily provoke shock. The experience of loss, whether through the death of a loved one or the ending of an intimate relationship, opens a place inside in which we enter into the core pain of our wounded child. It brings us up against not only our wounds, but also an emptiness in our being, which is at the root of our soul.

4) Condemnation or Criticism

Actually, this is a form of verbal violence. Most of us are so used to living with the fear and the experience of condemnation that we have taken it for granted. We don't realize how deeply it puts us into shock. Much of our behavior is oriented to avoiding criticism or reacting to it. Now the trauma of criticism, high expectations and criticism has gone deeply inside and becomes incorporated in a harsh inner critic. When faced with the threat of failure and receiving criticism, we can go deeply into shock, become dysfunctional and sabotage ourselves. Then the failure and criticism (from inside or outside of us) that we so feared become a self-fulfilling prophecy.

5) Mixed Messages

For instance, we are told that we should do whatever is best for us, with the underlying message to do what we are expected to do. Mixed messages such as these put us in deep shock because we can find no direction in which to go. And we stop trusting our own feelings. The child begins to see the outside world as a confusing and dangerous place in which nothing makes sense inside or outside of us.

6) Unpredictable, Irrational or Hysterical Behavior

Some years ago, I was in a relationship with someone who would get hysterical and abusive when angry or upset. I didn't know enough about the wounded child then to understand where this behavior was coming from or how I was provoking it. All I knew was I had to get away. I felt that I was going crazy inside. Nothing she said seemed to make any sense and nothing I said made any difference. It was a nightmare and I became paralyzed. Many clients and participants have shared with us similar kinds of experiences from childhood where one of their parents would react to them hysterically or irrationally. If a parent or parents were alcoholics, abused drugs or were highly emotional and unpredictable, we went into shock because we could not rely on any consistent behavior from them. We have lost our basic need for safety and security. Our world collapses.

The Effects of Shock – The Roots of Dysfunction

Shock can affect each of our energy centers and cause dysfunction in that area of our life. For instance, we can have *sexual shock* that deeply affects our ability to feel and open to our sexuality. Traumas from childhood, particularly sexual abuse, are often hidden deeply in our unconscious and can fill us with tremendous fear whenever we are confronted with a sexual situation. In our work, we have found that this kind of shock is almost universal and shows itself differently in each one of us. We can also have sexual dysfunction without having been sexually traumatized. It is simply that our shock shows itself in that area. Performance anxiety, problems related to orgasm, penetration, premature ejaculation and impotence are examples of shock revealing itself in the first energy center – the center of sexuality.

Shock can also show itself by filling us with profound *fears of survival*, obsessive thoughts and constriction in our behavior. A child whose early environment was full of fear of survival will have become infected with this fear and it can dominate his or her life as an adult, even if there is no longer a reason for these fears.

Abandonment shock can show itself as a dysfunction in the second center. The fear of rejection and abandonment that arises from early life experiences of being emotionally or physically abandoned can make it very difficult or us to feel emotion or to open and share ourselves. We pull back into our own world too afraid to run the risk of feeling the early pain of rejection. Again, this is often unconscious and we don't relate our difficulties with feeling our emotions to abandonment shock. It takes understanding of shock to realize that isolation is not our natural state.

Solar plexus shock is a shock to our ability to feel and express anger and assertiveness. This can arise from some form of physical or emotional violence, either overt or covert, that we sustained early in life. Now, the challenge of asserting ourselves can become crippling and terrifying. When we have been shocked in our solar plexus, it takes tremendous patience and perseverance to overcome the fear to feel and express ourselves assertively. When I first began to work on this aspect of my shock and began to take small risks to set limits and assert myself, my whole body would shake when I had to confront someone who frightened me. A deeper version of solar plexus shock is a difficulty of feeling our own uniqueness and sense of self.

We can have shock in the *heart center* causing us to become excessively serious and responsible. It is terrifying to allow ourselves to be playful and we may ever have forgotten how to be playful and joyful.

Shock can show itself in our *throat center* in difficulty expressing our creativity and articulating ourselves. It can feel as if the words and the energy actually get stuck in the throat. Perhaps as a child, we were unsupported, criticized, humiliated or patronized when we tried to express ourselves and now, faced with a challenge to express, we simply go into shock.

If we were looking into a mirror at this moment, we might detect, particularly in the left eye, the evidence of shock. We can detect a kind of blank stare. Our eyes are often the most obvious evidence of shock even if has become hidden and covered up by all the protection and defense that we fortunately built up. We can even see shock in the eyes of a person who seems to be functioning well in most areas of his or her life. Shock can have happened so early and was so devastating that there is often no connection to understanding. It is buried deeply in the unconscious. But once we become aware of shock, how it shows itself in the body and in our behavior, we begin to become more sensitive to it and to ourselves.

I remember an incident that happened years ago. At that time, I was only beginning to understand about my own shock. Some acquaintances of mine who also were living in the commune where I was living in India, had a regular gathering at their house in the evening. Because of the people who organized it, it was the "in" place to go at night. Even though I was somewhat intimidated by the people who ran it, I wanted to be included. One night, I was there and the hosts picked me for a "playful" teasing session. I went along with it but when I left, I felt as though I had been raped. I judged myself for not reacting and keeping my dignity. Now, I realize that I had gone into shock and in that state, no words ever come, let alone the right ones. In truth, I was already somewhat in shock before I even went because I didn't feel comfortable with this crowd, but did not trust myself enough to validate my own feelings. Shaming causes shock and shock leads to more shame. It becomes a vicious painful cycle.

Compensating for Feeling Our Terror

Under our shock state is terror. We may have learned to compensate for *feeling* terror in many of the same ways that we compensate for shame. We can recognize our ways of compensating by noticing the ways that we run away from feeling the panic inside. *Often, it is by speeding up, getting angry, spacing out or retreating deeply inside.* Just as with shame, it is

50

not always easy to connect with shock because most of us have been compensating for it all of our lives without realizing it. We never knew that the fear and anxiety we feel inside are signals that our vulnerability is in a state of shock. I think that our whole Western culture is in massive shock compensation. It is everywhere. Pressure and performance seem to be the dominant values of Western culture and the violence with which people relate to each other is ubiquitous and unconscious. All we have to do is read a newspaper or listen to a politician. Once we awaken to the world of our sensitivity and vulnerability, we can begin to see what we must be going through all the time. YEAH

How Shock Takes Us Away from Our Center

Shock cuts us off from ourselves. The pain is so great that we leave the body and lose touch with our energy. As a result, we are not in our center. When we are not in our center or in our energy, we feel a hole inside. This is not comfortable and so we look to fill the hole with something from the outside. That makes us co-dependent on other people, substances, activity, image, power and sex; anything to prevent us from feeling the profound panic inside.

Furthermore, when we are in shame or shock, we can't communicate or express ourselves clearly. When that happens, we get lost in the other person and we don't know who we are, what we want, or how we are feeling. We feel that without the other, we are helpless. We believe that we lack the resources to find ourselves. Our relationships become like emotional spaghetti, with a gradual loss of boundaries and identity. We try to compensate by cutting off, wanting more space, or demanding more energy from the other. We blame the relationship or the other person for the problems. The only way out of this nightmare is to begin healing the shock, by recognizing, staying with and feeling it.

The Gift of Compassion for Ourselves

There is no way that we can talk ourselves out of shock once it has been triggered. Many of us have experienced the frustration of seeing our energy and our performance deteriorate, watching ourselves sabotage and not being able to do anything about it. It is painful. If we are trying to accomplish something and we go into shock, then everything after that seems to go from bad to worse. The slightest bit of pressure from ourselves or from the outside takes us deeper into shock.

In relationship, usually one person has more shock than the other person, or at least more shock in certain areas than the other. If shock arises, for instance, in sexuality or in communication, the shock person normally will close down and retreat inside often without knowing why. The other person then feels abandoned and can become impatient and angry. It is fear facing fear, but the fear is experienced and expressed differently. This only heightens the other person's shock. This kind of downward spiral can happen in any situation where one person wants some kind of energy from the other. If we don't know about shock and begin to validate and work with the experience, it only creates more misunderstanding and distance.

By becoming aware of shock and being sensitive to how it feels when it comes up, I have learned to recognize when I am in shock. I don't always catch it right away, because it can happen so suddenly and unexpectedly, but I know what it feels like and I know that the feeling is shock. When it comes, there is nothing that I can do but stay with it, accept it, feel it and take a look at what triggered it.

Exercises: Accessing Shock:

Working with shock, focus on two things:

1) Shock in Your Life Today

- How does it affect your life today and what are your unique shock symptoms? *I shut down and don't wanna talk. Shaking hand, sweating palm hands. crying.*
- What triggers your shock? *Being fear of being rejected, judge. Confront causes shock.*
- What judgments do you have about yourself about being in shock? *I never got why I was feeling and acting like this. It was a big part of my life.*
- How do you compensate for the shock? *I don't know yet.*
- We suggest, as an exercise, that you list your own shock symptoms and discover what triggers your shock. Take a look at how you normally try to avoid feeling the shock and whatever judgments you have about being in shock.

2) Past Shock

Unraveling your shock history brings you tremendous compassion. But it is a process that is delicate and requires gentleness and patience and you might feel safer doing this with a professional who is trained in this area. When you explore your story, you can imagine that you are back in the environment of your childhood but now with the awareness, resources, strengths and understanding of an adult. Then you can ask:

- What in your early environment may have been shocking to you?

- What things about your mother or father could have been shocking to you?

- What circumstances in your early school environment might have been shocking?

- What message did you receive about what was expected of you?

Many people, while working with shock, begin to have memories and dreams of sexual and physical abuse, memories that they previously blocked from consciousness. Some of these memories

53

may be accurate and some can be confusing mixes of fact and extrapolation. But whatever comes up is significant, if not the exact memories, certainly the effects it has on your life today. Many of the most painful and traumatic childhood experiences remain lost to our memory and we must work with them very slowly and in a safe, supportive environment.

******

Chapter 5

The Wound of Abandonment –
From Anger and Grief toward Let Go and Bliss

Sometimes, we ask the participants of our workshops to share their biggest fear about opening to someone. For most people, it is the fear of rejection. We so much want to open - to another, to life - but we are afraid that if we do, we will get hurt. We have protected ourselves from being hurt and now when we open our vulnerability again, we want to know that we won't be hurt again. We don't want to have to feel that pain again; the pain of being betrayed, of being abandoned, of not getting our basic needs met and of having our heart damaged once again.

So here's the dilemma. We want to open but we don't want to get hurt. Unfortunately, existence offers no such guarantees.

On the contrary, if we open, the chances are we will feel abandoned, betrayed and deprived in some way. No matter how caring and present the other person is, he or she cannot possibly fill the holes that we have inside. We create experiences in life and in love that open this wound again and again and again, *because we have to go through the pain, deeply and thoroughly.* It seems to be the door to our depth and to a profound acceptance of our isolation. At the same time, the prospect of going into this pain is terrifying.

Abandonment Experiences Open Us to Inner Space

I can remember clearly the times in my life when I went through abandonment. I suspect that most of us can. My first time was just after graduating from university. I had been with a woman during the last two years of college and it was the first major relationship of my life. Prior to that, I did not have the slightest clue what it meant to come close to someone. She taught me patiently, but I think that I spent much of the time worrying about keeping my "freedom". After college, we were going to part

55

ways – she to law school and I to become a volunteer in the domestic Peace Corps. We both knew somehow that it was over, but when we separated, I went into a black hole. I had no understanding why it happened or what was happening, except that I felt utterly lost, lonely and desperate. It opened a space inside that seemed to have no relation to the actual events of the separation or even the relationship. It took me a full year to get back on my feet again emotionally, but I was not the same person after that experience. Something profound had shifted inside. It felt like for the first time, I was joining the human race. Before that, it felt like I was just going through the motions, not feeling anything and too concerned about getting on with things.

Years later, when I went through another such experience, I decided to work with a therapist. I uncovered feelings of deprivation originating in childhood that the breakup with my lover had triggered. This experience also brought me in touch with a space inside that was not psychological. It was a hollowness in my solar plexus that was new and frightening. I was waking up in the morning with a feeling of not knowing who I was. I knew about - and had experienced - dissociation and depression in the past, but this was different. I realized that I was entering a space that every seeker on the path of truth must go through, a space of feeling the void, the emptiness.

I continued to explore this space, bringing to it more acceptance and spaciousness. Understanding it and putting it into a spiritual context allowed me to go deeper into it and it created much more inner space. The uncomfortable feelings passed from this experience, as they had before, but again something seemed to have changed inside. For one thing, my fears are more on the surface and more easily triggered and there is also more space to stay vulnerable.

Abandonment and Deprivation – Different Doses of the Same Medicine

Life brings us these encounters with our wound of abandonment and emptiness all the time whether we like it or not. They come

56

in big or small doses and in different ways. It may come when a lover leaves us or when a loved one dies but it can also happen when whatever was providing meaning in our life no longer does. We also encounter our abandonment wound whenever we are not getting what we want, expect or think that we need from someone. This is a much less obvious and much more frequent encounter with abandonment. And we may not know that it is abandonment wound we are touching.

Whenever we have these experiences, we enter into a gap. It is space inside that has always been there usually covered with compensations and denial. When it finally opens, it can be anything from frustrating, irritating, disappointing or devastating. The terms abandonment, deprivation and emptiness are three ways that we can look at the same wound - three different ways that the hole inside can be opened. Each aspect gives greater depth of our understanding of this process.

Abandonment ✳

In some way, in our childhood, we have experienced being physically or emotionally abandoned. That pain was so overwhelming that we buried it deep in our unconscious. Our survival mechanisms were an attempt to recover from this assault. Our healing cannot happen, though, until we bring this early experience back to consciousness. We have to somehow re-open the wound. And the most common way we do this is in our intimate relationships. When we experience loss or rejection, we have re-created our abandonment wound. In fact, our fear of re-experiencing abandonment is the main reason why we avoid intimacy. Instead of running the risk, we keep our relating light, dramatic or conflictual. Unconsciously, we do anything to avoid opening our trust and having to go through the same betrayal that we felt as a child but have forgotten. It came as a surprise (and a revelation) to me to discover that my anti-dependent avoiding strategies were just a cover for this deep fear inside.

To our wounded inner child, (in other words – to the primal, often unconscious space inside) abandonment brings up the tremendous fears of not being provided for. When a lover leaves us, for example, or threatens to leave us, or when we suspect that he or she is attracted to another, we come face to face with the unconscious abandonment memories that we buried. To the child, it is not just the lover that may leave or has left, it feels that mother or father is gone or emotionally unavailable. It is not rational. And it is terrifying. It is as frightening to our inner child as it ever was. (Remember, our inner child is still back when the wound happened.) The fear shows itself in the body and can bring physical illness. It affects our dreams. It can cause so much disturbance in our regular life that we are afraid that we will not be able to cope. The more unconscious we are of the abandonment experience, the more it shows itself in body reactions.

When we experience rejection, we also have to deal with all the shame of unworthiness that is triggered. Both wounds hit us at once because they are so interconnected. I remember how tormented I have been during the abandonment crises in my life. My mind would run every judgment that it could think of and my body would be in panic. How often have we imagined our lover making love to someone else and comparing ourselves, always unfavorably, in every way? Every insecurity we have comes up and we are sure that each one is the gospel truth. Each time we see our ex-lover or his or her new lover, it becomes a nightmare of shame. Sometimes it can take months for the fear symptoms and the judging mind to quiet down.

But, I am convinced that on a higher level of our consciousness, we actually create abandonment crises to take us deeper. As seekers of truth, the experience of abandonment takes on a totally new perspective. To our child, it is abandonment, but to our seeker, it is an entrance into a void that we all have to face sooner or later. Facing it can open a deep space of trust and the beginning to surrender.

Deprivation ✳

Deprivation is a form of abandonment but in smaller doses. It is a more chronic form of not getting what we want or expect. When someone doesn't listen to us when we are speaking, or when we are not given time, attention, support or touch, it is deprivation. Each of us has our own special deprivation wound depending on the way in which we experienced not getting what we needed as a child. If we want to know what our deprivation story is, all we have to do is ask ourselves what it is today in our life that makes us feel betrayed or deprived of love. My biggest deprivation wound is not feeling seen, respected and recognized, or feeling controlled and manipulated instead of supported. I can directly relate that to my early life issues. *my biggest deprivation wound is when someone doesn't listen to me.*

We will re-create our own particular deprivation pattern in all of our significant relationships. Our lovers (and close friends) will, one way or another, treat us much the same way that we were treated as a child. They will deprive us in much the same way. "How could they do that?" we say. "After all, they are supposed to be loving, not depriving us." But in the same way that we are compelled to reenact our abandonment, we have to do the same with deprivation. Our lover may not have left us, but within the relationship, we reenact our deprivation story. If we don't recognize this, it can make us furious, depressed or crazy.

There is a profound lesson hidden in deprivation experiences. *Intimacy involves continual encounters with deprivation.* In the challenge of a committed, long-term and deepening relationship with anyone, friend or lover, we are continually faced with the frustration of not getting what we want. Does that mean that the other person is not the "right one", or needs to change? Perhaps, but no matter whom we relate with deeply, we are going to get frustrated and disappointed sooner or later. When we are in the middle of feeling deprived, convinced that we are not getting what we "need", we have only two choices. We can choose to leave the relationship, which is always our freedom, or, *we can choose to go inside and feel the deprivation/abandonment wound that has just been opened.* But it is not a choice to try and change the other person; it makes the other person pull away more and, most importantly, it is a strategy not to feel our own pain and frustration.

I represent this choice in a simple drawing. Imagine three circles one inside the other and one in the middle. *In the outer circle, we are focused on the outer and on the other person.* We are trying to change the outer or use some distraction to escape from the feelings. The outer circle represents all our avoidance of feeling, our escape mechanisms, which includes our entitlement strategies of revenging, passively aggressing, dumping, controlling, belittling, judging, blaming, dumping, raging, threatening, cutting off, pulling away, playing the victim, creating conflict and giving up. The outer circle also represents our addictions and resignation.

In the middle circle, we encounter the abandonment wound. Our focus is no longer directed out trying to manipulate the outside circumstances or person to relieve our anxiety. We have made the choice to feel and with that choice, we also invite the feelings associated with this wound; frustration, anxiety and panic, emptiness, loneliness, despair, helplessness, desperation, the hurt and pain of separation, even our anger at God or Existence. In the outer circle, we are involved in the endless effort to control or change the outside world so that we don't have to feel pain. Inside, we accept and feel it.

Finally, the center of the circle represents what happens once we surrender to the abandonment wound and are willing to feel. *We are rewarded with profound feelings of expansion, relaxation, let go and even bliss.* Not right away and not according to our expectations and our timetable, but it happens.

Often, it takes life handing us a big dose of the wound before we finally make the choice to go in and feel. When our lover is frustrating us, for example and not meeting our conscious or unconscious expectations, we may cling to the hopes that he or she will change. We alternate between periods of hope and despair. There is still someone to project our frustrations onto. We

60

can blame and continue the delusion that in time something will change with the other person. Often with this kind of deprivation, we never consciously face the pain. If we finally lose hope of changing the other person, we start fresh with another and the game begins all over again.

But when we are hit with a big dose of the wound, when a loved one rejects us or dies, life has given us an experience where we can no longer avoid feeling the wound. We are forced to feel it. There is no escape. The fear can be almost overwhelming. It is my experience that it is the fear and not the pain that is so hard to face. Once I have survived the fear, I have somehow created space inside to feel the pain of the loss and the shame that comes with it. But to overcome the fear, I have needed support and guidance.

Facing deprivation has always been one of my biggest challenges. I like to analyze people and tell them what is wrong with them so that they can change for me. My first and almost compulsive reaction has been to get on the other person's case, particularly Amana, and in my mind, I am absolutely convinced that I am right. It feels a bit like a dog not wanting to let go of a bone. Fortunately, Amana doesn't buy into it at all. Whenever I go down the road of letting her know what is wrong with her and how she should change, she throws it right back in my face. I struggle for a while trying to get her to see the "truth", until I finally give up and take the time to feel the wound. (And to give myself some credit, sometimes I get it right away.) When we are finally so in love with someone that we don't even consider the option of leaving, we have no choice but to feel the wound. Perhaps that is one of the most wonderful qualities of a deep relationship.

Emptiness ✺

Lying under the psychological experiences of abandonment and deprivation – the reenactment of our childhood pain – is the experience of emptiness. This also gets triggered when we go through a loss. It is the space of the void where we experience a profound loss of meaning in our life. This experience seems to be waiting for us as we go deeper because we cling for meaning to so many insubstantial things. When they start to crumble, it creates a terrifying gap. I know that I am quite attached to my roles and too many ingredients of my self-image, but in penetrating moments, I can see how shallow they are. I also keep myself very busy and occupied. Some of it is genuine enthusiasm for my creativity and my aliveness, but some of it is a cover for feeling the void.

The path inside naturally and inevitably takes us away from our attachment to roles, to material entanglements and to being busy and forces us into the void. This can bring much fear because we often have not yet found anything else to replace it. My spiritual master spoke repeatedly that, on the path of meditation, we must go through this space if we want to get free. It is what mystics have called, "the dark night of the soul". In these moments, my ongoing connection to my master and his teachings have been the most important support I have had, because my experience of him was that he had genuinely been through the dark spaces and constantly encouraged me to keep going in spite of the pain and difficulties.

Shadows of the Abandonment Wound

The abandonment wound is the shadow behind our disappointments. But when we are not aware of this, we can easily get lost in complaint and blame and believe what our mind is saying. I would like to share one poignant example of this from my own life. In 1990, my spiritual master died. At that time, I had been connected to him and his commune intimately for over ten years. His death was a shock for many of us who had been deeply involved in this path, but on the whole, my sense was that we were not in touch with the depth of the shock and how it would show itself in our lives.

As a group, there was no collective acknowledgement of the connection between his death and the primal abandonment wound. The prevailing themes were, "There is no such thing as death", "He gave us everything we need and now we can move on our own" and so on - all true but missing something. People's pain of abandonment wound began to show itself in indirect ways; continual complaints about how the commune was being run in his absence, feeling betrayed that he left so soon, reminiscing about the past and bitterness about the whole experience with the master. I had some of all of these reactions, but it helped me to understand that all of it was coming because primal abandonment feelings were being triggered. Whenever we come close to someone and experience a loss, the wound is opened and beckons us to feel it.

Our Seeker, Not Our Child, Can Work with Our Wounds

When we are taken over by the consciousness of our wounded child (a theme that I will take up in the next chapter), we do not have the resources to handle and process wounds. We just panic and want to run away from the discomfort as quickly and as effectively as possible. When our wounds are triggered – shame, shock or abandonment, we need to connect with another space inside, a space that we could call "the inner seeker", which does have the know-how to deal with them. This part of us can provide the space, clarity and distance to cope with the intense fears that arise. It carries the understanding for what is happening and how important it is for our inner growth. Our seeker helps us to choose, not move immediately, habitually and unconsciously into the panic and reactiveness of our panicked child.

When our lover or life doesn't meet our expectations, usually, the first thing we do is react; blame and complain, or collapse and sink into resignation. Under that reaction is much anger, frustration and perhaps a sense of despair and hopelessness. These feelings are triggered by our experiencing deprivation and abandonment. In fact, this is the source of many, if not most, of the conflicts that come up between lovers. Jealousy, at its root, is nothing more than a rekindling of the memory of being left. For example, you are having a beautiful connection with your lover and then for some reason, his or her energy is pulled away. You feel deprived and react. The deprivation that is occurring in the moment triggers the deprivation that you experienced in the past. The wound is triggered. It comes up frequently, for instance, when we are not getting our sexual needs or expectations met. Sexual needs touch primal feelings inside.

I recently did a session with a couple who were dealing with this kind of issue. She was hurt and angry because in making love, she felt that he was being insensitive. He was angry because whenever she complained, he felt his flow and his energy being cut off. Exploring more deeply, it turned out that she had suffered sexual abuse as a child and when she felt that he was moving too fast, her wound was triggered. From his side, he had been dominated by a highly controlling mother with high expectations and when she stopped him and complained that he was not being sensitive, he felt controlled and criticized. They were triggering each other's wounds.

To a child who is helpless, innocent and totally dependent, every abuse, every intolerance and every lack of attention is experienced as abandonment. We experience that there is no one there to provide for our basic needs. That creates panic. Even though we are now adult and realistically can take care of these basic needs, when the wound opens, our child only remembers a former time where there was devastating fear. That is the reason that we avoid opening this wound.

It is often difficult to trace the source of this wound. For those of us who were actually physically abandoned by one or both parents, or for those of us who were physically or sexually abused, the cause is more obvious. But for others, it may not be so clear. I had much difficulty identifying the source of my deprivation until I entered therapy and over the years, I have slowly discovered areas of deeply traumatic deprivation at each major developmental stage.

For the purposes of healing our wounded child, it is not so important to discover how it happened. But it is important to recognize that it did happen and to recognize its ramifications in our life today, particularly in our relationships. To be sure, the intensity of the panic and the abandonment varies for each of us, but basically we are all in the same boat. Some of us may have found more efficient ways of covering up, denying and compensating for our wound, but we all carry it. To feel it instead of running away from it requires tremendous courage.

Facing the Wound

I offer some suggestions that have helped me to work with the abandonment wound:

1) Framing

This is recognition that when we feel frustrated, disappointed or in despair, our abandonment wound has been triggered and this is existence's way of bringing it to our attention so that we can heal it.

Basically, the abandonment wound is the main source of all of our co-dependency issues. Our reactiveness and entitlement – our strategies, our efforts to control, dominate and manipulate the other – are nothing more than a cover for our wound of abandonment. This understanding brings about a radical change in how we relate. Unconsciously, we are hoping that we will eventually find someone who will meet all the needs that were not met as a child. Our adult may recognize rationally that this is not possible, but our child never relinquishes this hope. And this hope is then projected, mostly unconsciously, onto our lover and life in general. The abandonment wound is triggered at the moment when we begin to feel that our needs are not being met.

From my experience, it is extremely helpful to know that all of these feelings are nothing more than the abandonment wound and that we cannot heal what we cannot feel and understand. To our child, what is happening in the present is a real abandonment. It cannot distinguish the trigger from the source. When it happened, it was much too devastating to feel. When the pain is triggered now, it seems to our child inside to have the same intensity. But we are no longer a child and now we have the resources to heal.

2) Accepting and giving space to the fear and pain

The more inviting we are to face the wound when it arrives, the easier it is to get through it. As long as our expectations of life don't include dealing with this wound, we are asking for trouble. If we are using relationships to avoid feeling this emptiness, it will never work; we are using relationships to run away from ourselves. If we live with the attitude that pain is not part of life, we invite suffering rather than healing and there is no space to go through the fear and feel our pain when it comes. This is most acute in relationships because, conditioned to believe in the romantic fantasy, we believe, unconsciously perhaps, that our lover will give us what we did not get as a child. Actually, our higher consciousness has something totally different in mind. It wants us to be free and the only way that we can become free is to go through the fear and pain of abandonment, deprivation and emptiness.

Once the relationship has passed through the honeymoon where all is wonderful and our lover is the incarnation of all our greatest needs and desires, we are headed inevitably for disappointment. It can be in sex, in intimacy, in spontaneity, in intelligence, in spirituality, in any number of ways. This is when the trouble starts. For a time, we may live in denial, or accommodate, but underneath, we are building resentment. This resentment can be expressed in many indirect ways – in sarcasm, in criticism and judgments, or in subtle acts of revenge. All the while, the relationship becomes more and more bitter. We find ourselves complaining about our lover to friends, or we may express the resentment directly in the form of physical or emotional abuse. Perhaps we eventually leave the relationship, fully convinced that we needed to leave because that person could not meet our needs.

We are missing to recognize that every relationship will provoke our deprivation and abandonment in some way. No one can fill our holes inside. Experiencing the pain of abandonment and deprivation with awareness is precisely how we can slowly fill our holes. It can help us to accept our aloneness. Our first encounters with aloneness are often experienced as deprivation.

Disappointment and frustration in life is always staring us in the face, particularly in our relationships. Existence is not there to meet our expectations but to get us free. We are often stubborn and resistant. Intimacy brings nourishment but it also brings pain. Only once we are willing to face this fully can we begin to find some harmony in our love life and to find some grace in how we navigate through life. Healing this wound is the door to our deeper self. Until our deprivation wound is healed and we have learned to accept our aloneness thoroughly, we cannot be free. Recognizing this helps us not to fight so much when the wound is opened.

3) Reaching out for support

When the wound is opened, there can be extreme anxiety. Sometimes, the darkness and loneliness seem bottomless, never ending and there is a fear that we will go mad or kill ourselves. We can feel deeply depressed, become highly self-critical and the overall negativity and loss of trust can darken all our waking hours. The more severe the trigger, the stronger are these symptoms. It has helped me in these times to risk reaching out to get nourishment, not expecting anyone to take the pain away, but just to feel not so alone. Many of us suffer our pain in isolation and fortify our belief that we have to face our pain alone. This is a false kind of aloneness based on contraction rather than expansion, based on fear and mistrust rather than trust. There is a voice inside that says, "No one can be here for me when I feel like this", or "I'm a burden" and so on. But our healing comes precisely from reaching out when we are hurting. Once I found the courage to reach out, much of the fear dissipated.

4) A little help from meditation

A simple technique of taking some moments to sit down and breathe slowly seems to help develop an awareness inside that the painful period will pass. This pain has come before and it passed. This time, it also will pass. Also, it has been my experience that each time we go through it, it gets easier. Each time I have gone through the pain, I am more resourceful, not so isolated and there is more space inside to feel and be with the anxiety and pain.

From Loneliness to Aloneness

Facing abandonment, deprivation and emptiness whether little or big ones, is facing our loneliness, facing that space inside where we feel very alone in the universe, unprotected, unloved and uncared for. It is a black hole that we don't really want to enter. When I am in the abandonment pain, I'm not feeling the joy and freedom of aloneness, at least not at first. I am in fear and pain, the pain that I so artfully avoided by being anti-dependent. Opening to love invites the pain of loss. It is safer to stay closed and never have to experience this pain. But then we live without love. It hurts either way. If we go through it, it resolves; if we don't, it lingers all of our life. There is no way to avoid the pain of love.

Fundamentally, we all have a deep longing inside to be filled, to be whole. The pain of abandonment and deprivation simply opens this deep longing inside that normally we project onto a lover. No lover can contain or satisfy that longing. That longing is the deepest part of our being because we are longing to return to the source. It is at the heart of our spiritual search and mistakenly gets directed to another person. Abandonment triggers this longing. We often feel the longing as a frightening loneliness, but this loneliness is a period of transition between feeling this loneliness and eventually coming to enjoy our aloneness and rediscovering an inner bliss and trust in life. Instead of feeling universal love and a mystical sense of place and purpose in life, what comes at first, usually, are waves of intense heaviness and darkness. Had we not suffered abandonment as a child, this probably would not happen. But we did and so we have to go through this transition period.

Facing our loneliness is one of the places where the spiritual path loses its romantic and idealistic fantasies. When this wound comes up, we are in the trenches. It hurts and every part of our conscious mind wants to avoid feeling the pain. Until we are

68

willing to face this wound, we meet pain, disappointment, and frustration with anger and expectation. Our journey through life cannot be deep or blissful and our relationships will develop into superficial arrangements covering mountains of resentment. But once we pull back the projection that another will fill us, we can actually share the path of finding truth with another. Until then, the lover is not yet a friend; he or she is someone we project upon to relieve our pain.

EXERCISE – Working with the Abandonment Wound

Imagine a recent situation where you felt deprived or abandoned – a situation in life, with your lover or even a close friend where somehow you were not getting what you wanted.

- What was the trigger of the upset? In what way did you feel deprived or abandoned? What did you not get that we expect to get? In sex, communication, openness, energy, money, support, guidance, warmth, touch, sensitivity?

- How you responded to the frustration?

- What kind of strategies did you use to try and get the other to change – blame, manipulation, revenge, control, complain, analyze?

- Did you go into resignation?

- What are the underlying feelings - sadness, anger, despair and hopelessness?

******

Part 2

The Child State of Consciousness
and How It Runs Our Life

Chapter 6

Reatividade   Direito

Reactiveness, Entitlement and Magical Thinking –
Qualities of the Child State of Consciousness

Because of early traumas of one kind or another, for many of us, our natural aliveness, spontaneity, trustfulness, innocence and joy has been covered by a layer of mistrust, insecurity and fear. Prior to our choosing to face and work with our fears and insecurities, our consciousness easily gets taken over by our panicked child. This part of us knows no way to deal with the fear other than to use all its intelligence and energy to try and make it go away. It acts and reacts from fear. This part of our consciousness has no ability to feel the fear; it simply wants to get rid of it as fast and as efficiently as possible.

We call this space, *"the child state of consciousness"*. This consciousness is fear and shame based; it is emotional, reactive and full of expectations. To compensate for the panic, we become political. Our energy gets directed outward – to meet the needs of the child anyway we can. To do that, we become manipulative, controlling, demanding, vengeful, calculating, cunning, pleasing, raging or whatever works best. We have developed and perfected these strategies since childhood. In addition to being reactive, entitled and emotional, in the child state of consciousness, we also dream, fantasize and idealize rather than look at reality directly.

Like any child not getting what he or she wants, we act out. *That's the reactive part.* And we do it with the feeling that we deserve to get it. *That's the entitled part.* Plus, rather than see and face reality as it is, we blindly hope for life to give us what we want and to be treated as we hope to be. *That's the magical part.* In the child state of consciousness, we are focused on survival – charged with the belief that we must act urgently to get what we need. Without it, we will not make it. In the consciousness of this child, we have learned to live with a jungle mentality of competition and struggle. We are charged with anger, fear and urgency; we want what we want and we want it now. We see and react to the outside entirely as though we were looking out through the eyes of a deprived and panicked child who must satisfy his needs urgently.

Acting Out from the Child State of Consciousness

From a very early age, we learned that there was no one to take care of our deepest needs except ourselves. We became the vigilant protectors of our panicked child. With our attention and our senses focused outward, we learned how to control and manipulate our environment the best way we could to try and keep safe. For many of us, if not most of us, it seemed like a matter of life and death. Naturally, dependent on the kind and extent of the abuse we suffered, each one of us developed a different style of reaction with different intensity, strategies, and styles. In this energy, we have a vigilance to protect our vulnerable side from feeling pain, fear, disappointment, or loss at all costs.

When I began to explore my own reactive child, I was shocked and embarrassed at what I found – so full of mistrust, hurt, anger and defensiveness. Deep inside, I have carried the belief that no one is ever going to be there. The slightest disappointment causes me to pull back into my familiar cave. I pull back with unexpressed anger, pulling back to hurt the other for not giving me what I want. My deepest expectation is that my lover or close friends should understand me intuitively and always be sensitive to me without my having to say anything. When this isn't the case, I feel betrayed and angry.

From our child's perspective, survival did depend on whatever strategies and protection we developed. The world is a place in which we get what we need by demanding, manipulating and controlling. We calculate what will get us what we want from the other person. We can play a rescuer, controlling and manipulating people by making them dependent on us and indebted to us. We can play a victim, controlling others by making them feel sorry and guilty, or we can play a tyrant, by simply overpowering and

74

controlling with fear. We behave as any child would to get what he or she wants, or react as a child when he doesn't get what he wants. Except now, with the sophisticated mind of an adult, we can be a monster. We expect, blame, complain, demand, manipulate, rage, pout, whine and plot revenge. We attack with physical, verbal, or sexual violence. We can cut off with a righteous indignation or launch into criticism and judgment and we feel fully justified in our behavior. We cannot see that our behavior is fueled with resentments for past hurts and the panic of not getting what we need.

All of our behavior that shows lack of respect for other persons, such as showing up late without considering or caring that we have kept someone waiting, eating food off the plates of friends without asking, expecting others to pay for us or forgetting about money that we owe them, leaving messes around so someone else will clean them up, *comes out of the child state of consciousness.* We complain about things not being how we want them to be but are not willing to take responsibility to change them. We get irritated when something is too difficult, we allow other people to do the work, and then blame others for it not being how we want it to be.

All this covers up the deep fears and vulnerability inside. We are filled with resentment for not getting our needs met and get angrily disappointed when, for one reason or another, our expectations are not fulfilled. At that moment of disappointment we actually feel abandoned and it triggers all the disappointments we felt as a child when we were not loved, understood, accepted and approved. But rather than feel the pain, we react and blame. The core of our reactiveness is the unwillingness to feel the fear and the pain of having our expectations disappointed.

The Child State of Consciousness in Relationship

When we begin to understand about the child state of consciousness, we can bring light to much of the conflicts that occur in intimate relationships. When our needs and wants conflict with another's, we enter in a primal state of fear that we won't get what we need. Instead of communicating, we react. I recall a session with a couple who were having much conflict in their love life. She felt that he was often insensitive and invasive while he felt controlled by her telling him how he should be. They could not listen to each other. They could not go beneath the conflict because without an understanding for what is going on, all they could see was that the other was a threat to their panicked child.

The only way out of such a dilemma, from our experience, is to begin to explore our child state of consciousness and ask ourselves:

• What fears lie behind my expectations and reactions?

• What am I feeling?

• What am I wanting?

Normally, we don't take the time or the interest to ask ourselves these questions and go deeper. We just react. Unfortunately, because our trust has been so deeply damaged, we express our needs with the charge of expectation and the fear that they will never be met. We are guarded and mistrustful. This charge of expectation unfortunately reinforces our experience and belief that our needs will not be met because we push other people away. The result is that we do not get the love and support we need and that makes our fear and charge even worse. This is the tension that creates so much conflict and drama between lovers and generally so much misery in our life.

When we enter into a relationship, we seldom have much clue of what lies ahead. Here's a possible scenario: We meet someone and fall in love. Two adults have fallen in love, but underneath, there is an entirely different drama beginning to brew. On the surface, we operate with the best intentions to give and receive love, to share, to communicate and to nurture. Yet, inside each of us is also a wounded child with strong needs for love and a vast world of hidden fears and expectations. Once in a relationship, this child starts to surface. He (or she) looks out, and says to himself, "Hum, there is someone out there who is saying, 'I love you'. Is that possible?" This child inside is probably not used to being loved, truly loved. Naturally, he is a bit skeptical. "Could it be," our child says to himself, "that this person really loves me? Let's check it out."

We have a basket in which are stored all the needs that were never met as a child. Generally, we have stored this basket deep in the basement and forgotten about it. In fact, we may not even know what a need is anymore. But being in love starts to bring back memories of the basket and with these memories arise all the secret longings to be loved that we stored in that basket. So, (unconsciously), we take a little trip to the basement and start looking for the basket. Finding it, we say to ourselves, "Hey, this person says she loves me. So let's test it out. I'll try need number 8." (Need number 8 isn't such a big one.)

Since it is such a little need, our lover will most likely be more than happy to meet it. After all, that is what love is about, isn't it? Then our lover reaches into her basket and pulls out one of hers. This game can go on for quite a while. The more familiar and comfortable we get with rummaging around our basket and the more familiar we get with the other person, the more our expectations grow. After all, we have been waiting all of our life to have these needs met. Eventually, we start reaching for the really big ones such as: "I really want you to be there for me all the time", or, "I want you to give me the space I need, but I don't want you to leave me or see anyone else."

Unfortunately, all this communication is unconscious and indirect. Slowly our feelings of disappointment and betrayal grow. We may not even know that we have expectations, but we can sense a growing feeling of frustration, pain and disappointment. Each of us reacts differently to this disappointment. We may cut off and pull away, blame, get bitchy or abusive. In time, we place on our lover all the unmet needs we never got from mommy or daddy. Then the trouble starts, because deep inside, we expect that love means that we should get them met and that the other person should shelter us from our fears and pain. That is love, we think. Two unconscious children both with their fears, their unmet needs, demands and expectations interacting with each other create pure havoc. These two wounded needy children face each other, neither able to understand nor meet the needs of the other.

They approach each other, not with vulnerability, but with entitlement. We can go for years carrying the load of all our fears and unfulfilled needs, denying and minimizing them but unconsciously holding onto the expectation that someday they will be met. As soon as we have developed some trust with someone, we believe that because we have opened, the other person is supposed to satisfy our needs. It is as though in this situation, we are wearing a pair of glasses that cloud our vision. What we see through these glasses is no longer our lover, but a projection of the parent we never had and desperately want. However, expectation is like skunk oil. Paradoxically, instead of meeting the needs of our inner child, *our entitlement and reactiveness only succeeds at pushing away the love that we so deeply need, making us even more desperate and panicked.*

The Child State of Consciousness Does Not Understand Boundaries

Later, I will explore the issue of boundaries much more deeply. But now, I want to point out how this topic relates to the child state of consciousness. In the child state of consciousness, we have little understanding or appreciation for respecting boundaries – our own and those of others. It comes from not having our space and integrity respected as a child. Unconsciously in the grips of our fear, we violate our own space because of the terror of being rejected, invaded, abused or disapproved of. Or we violate another's space because we are so blinded by our panic to get our needs met that we cannot see anything except what we want. And in relationships, we both invade and get invaded all the time.

78

1) Being Invaded

We often don't even know what it is like to respect ourselves enough to set limits and let others know if our space is being invaded. As a child, we were not able to build up enough self-esteem and self-dignity to respect our space and let people know when we were being invaded. In our workshops, when we discuss the many ways we allow our boundaries to be abused, people are often astonished that it is something they have a right to protect. Inside there is a belief that we don't deserve space and we continually shrink our energy, making ourselves smaller, denying ourselves or apologizing for ourselves. It is a painful state and one that builds up tremendous inner resentment.

Deep inside, we know that we are not allowing ourselves to live our potential. We are so afraid to expand lest we meet rejection, anger or lack of understanding. When we are being invaded, it is easy to blame the other person for being entitled and insensitive without seeing our own entitlement. It took me a long time to see that in this situation, the person being invaded is a victim. He or she has an unspoken and often unconscious expectation that his space should be respected without him having to say or do anything.

Claude is a good example of someone who easily allows his space to be invaded. He has found that respecting his own needs is one of his biggest problems whenever he gets close to anyone, especially in his most intimate relationships. Although extremely creative and energetic, he is shy and self-effacing with people and gets easily overpowered. He finds that with his lovers, he overextends himself in trying to be sensitive to their desires. In this process of trying to give them what they want, he loses touch with his own needs. He is terrified of the reaction of the other person, particularly of her getting angry or rejecting him.

After being with someone for a while, he starts feeling resentful that she is not more sensitive to him and even begins to feel betrayed. He can't understand why the other person doesn't love him enough to be sensitive to what he wants and needs without his always having to say it. He resents giving so much and always being taken advantage of. He sees himself repeating this pattern over and over. His conclusion has been that he just has to have more trust and faith in people and eventually they will respect his feelings more. (A long wait.)

2) Invading

On the other extreme, when we are taken over by the panicked child (which can be a chronic condition), we can be a massive space invader. We simply run over other people to get what we want – believing it is either get or be gotten. This belief is deeply buried in an unconscious fear of survival and is generally covered up with social niceties. Often we may not even be aware that we are being aggressive and violent in our behavior toward others.

Carla is a classic example of an entitled space invader. A 29-year-old tall, blonde, attractive woman, she has an imposing and magnetic energy but uses her sexuality and her assertiveness to get what she wants. People find her appealing and exciting to be with; they are drawn to her sexuality, energy and power but are also mistrustful of her manipulativeness. She requires much space to expand, but she is generally not sensitive to others' space or needs and tends to overpower people without realizing it. When someone finds the fortitude to object, she blames them for being repressed and uptight. She has little awareness about how she uses her power and sex to control. She judges others for being too weak or emotional, only because she is terrified that if she allows her own vulnerability to surface, she will not survive in the world and will be dominated and controlled by others. She notices that people complain about her behind her back and her lovers object to her toughness and insensitivity. She herself keeps finding reasons to blame them for not understanding her.

Our Reactiveness and Entitlement are Saboteurs

It is very difficult for us to see and feel our own reactive entitled child. We can see and feel it in others, but are very reluctant to turn the mirror on ourselves. But an understanding for this part of us is essential because it undermines our life. *When we relate with reactiveness and entitlement, we sabotage love, self-respect and inner growth.* We sabotage love because our attitude and behavior is basically self-centered and disrespectful of the other. We sabotage our self-respect because deep down, we know that when we are acting from entitlement, we are not honoring ourselves or anyone else. And we sabotage our inner growth because in this space, we are focused entirely on the outside – on getting what we want from the outside, or on blaming the outside for what we don't get.

The Magical/Regressed Child

I have an acquaintance who is continually finding new growth paths. Each one is the ultimate solution for all emotional and life problems. Each new teacher that he finds is the one he has always been waiting for, the one who has the ultimate wisdom and all the answers to his burning questions. Periodically, he calls me to fill me in on his latest discovery, launches into a passionate discourse about all the attributes of his new teacher. Then after a while when he starts to see the limitations of his latest fling, he tires, loses interest and moves on.

I can relate to a similar tendency in myself. Our natural enthusiasm, innocence and trust is beautiful, but it is also naïve. In the child state of consciousness, we easily fall into the space of magical thinking. The magical child inside of us is forever searching for something or something to look up to, to idealize, to give our power and responsibility away to - whether it is a teacher, a guru, a boss, a therapist, a lover or a friend. In the child state of consciousness, we do not believe that we have the confidence, resources or intelligence to make our own decisions, to trust our own thoughts, feelings and intuition. And with that mentality, we easily become susceptible to influence and control by another person.

The magical child also has a blind and childish trust in people and in life, which again is endearing, but it is not in harmony with reality. It does not want to look at the fact that the world is not as he or she imagines it should be. It is a painful awakening to accept the world and other people with all the insensitivity, unconsciousness and violence that exists. In our hope that people should be as our magical child would like them to be, we feel endlessly betrayed. And it robs us of our power and self-respect when we are wearing pink glasses imagining the world to be like a fairy tale, or when are continually giving our power away to someone else who can give us answers. In the child state of consciousness, we seek lovers to take away our fears of loneliness, we seek teachers to give us answers and take away our fears and we project onto others the competence and confidence that we wish we had ourselves. The problem is not that we have lovers, therapists or gurus, but if we relate to them from our child state of consciousness, we stay a child, disempowered and dependent.

As a second child, I know well what it is like to hold someone higher than myself and project onto that person one's own longings. As early as junior high school, I was already bragging about my older brother and earning self-esteem from his qualities while disregarding my own. I always felt that my brother's opinion was infallible and that he could achieve whatever he wanted to. I got into the habit of asking him about everything. I didn't realize until much later that I was robbing myself of my dignity by doing this because, in the comparison, I was strengthening my sense of dependency and deficiency and I was unable to appreciate my own uniqueness and strength. I can now appreciate that this kind of comparison strengthened my own mystification and magical thinking.

When we open to something new, it is natural that we bring to it a childish enthusiasm and innocent trust. But unless we bring with us our own intelligence, we get lost into idealizing another and never learn to develop our own intuition and resourcefulness. When we look up to someone, we can easily regress into a dependent and disempowered state, which continually robs us of self-respect. Furthermore, when we hold onto magical dreams and hopes, we are not learning to deal with the painful realities of life. We are not learning to build containment for frustration and

82

disappointment and learning to face life as it is rather than as we want it to be. The process of learning to face reality builds immense inner strength.

In the next few chapters, I will be exploring in more detail how the child state of consciousness comes up in our relating. As long as it remains unconscious, it can run our life and create havoc. When we bring it to consciousness, we can use it as a source of growth and self-awareness.

******

Chapter 7

Expectations -
The Fuel of Reaction and Entitlement

In the child state of consciousness, we are an expecting machine. In fact, if we look closely, we can recognize that the fuel of our entitlement comes from our expectations. Expectations come directly from our child state of consciousness. As we mature and gain perspective from this kind of consciousness, we see that expectations have nothing to do with reality. Life is as it is and people are as they are. We can expect as much as we want, but neither life nor people pander to our expectations. It is only our child way of thinking that has expectations.

We all have expectations of each other, but it is important that we recognize them for what they are – an aspect of the child state of consciousness.

Otherwise, we invite suffering into our life and we will destroy whatever harmony and intimacy we wish to create. Expectations turn life or the other person into an object for our wants. This effectively blocks the deeper inner space of trust and gratitude to grow. Instead of feeling our fear, we move into the entitled child and feel victimized by people, situations and life.

Uncovering Our Expectations

It is not always so easy to get in touch with our expectations. First of all, we don't want to admit that we even have them. At least, that it how it has been for me. I'm such a spiritual guy. Intellectually, I understand that I am alone. But when someone disappoints me, I could kill. So much for my "understanding". I am full of expectations. I expect that people give to me as much as I give to them. I expect that people always be fair with me, especially my good friends. I expect that those close to me will be truthful, reliable and understanding. And the list goes on.

How do we recognize our expectations? One way is to notice when we feel disappointed and react. When we feel disappointed, we may blame, get angry or cut off and go into resignation. Anger and resignation are simply two sides of the coin of unfulfilled expectations. Depending on our temperament, we can throw the anger and disappointment on the other person for not meeting our needs, or we take it inside and stew on it; we explode or we implode. It is embarrassing to see how much we expect. That's why we don't want to look at it. Whenever we feel disappointment or anger, an expectation was not met. What was it?

Another doorway to uncover our expectations is by *examining what lies underneath our judgments.* Often, just behind a judgment is something that we want or expect from someone. I have found this a highly fruitful way for me to discover my expectations, because often I can be so righteous in my judgments that I don't go deep enough to examine what wound is being triggered.

A third way of discovering an expectations is by *looking at our blame and complaining.* Whenever we blame or complain, there is some expectation underneath that has not been met. We complain about someone's behavior, expecting it to be different, or we complain about the weather, politics, friends or authority – always with the hidden expectation that something should change.

Finally, another window to expectations comes from *looking at different areas of your life.* For instance, what expectations do we have about sex? How would we like to be made love to, to be touched, how often would we like this to happen and how do we want to be approached? What would we like to experience in the other person while making love or in ourselves? How would we like someone to be there for us emotionally? Are they as present, sensitive, wild, patient, energetic, alive, kind, generous, perceptive and attentive as we would like? Is our lover or friend intensive enough in his or her search for truth, confident, centered, meditative, silent, self-contained or powerful enough for

86

us? Is he or she as joyful, creative and positive about life as we would like?

Since we will never find anyone who satisfies all our expectations, every relationship gives us an opportunity to explore them. The closer we come, the greater our expectations. A client recently shared in a group that he had tons of expectations on his girlfriend, but lately he noticed that he was not so disturbed by her "deficiencies" as before. We asked him if anything had changed in their relating and he said that he had taken distance and was not seeing her as often as before. *When the child does not get its expectations met, it either gets angry or retreats.* In neither case, are we dealing with the root. When we respond to frustration and disappointment only with anger or resignation, we remain in the child state of consciousness. The only way that we mature beyond this state of consciousness is by connecting with and feeling the wound under the expectations.

Feeling What is Behind Our Expectations

When we explore these expectations, *we can also notice how we feel in our body with each one as it comes up;* some may have a mild charge, others a very strong one. Expectations cover up a hole inside. But instead of feeling the fear and pain connected to this emptiness, we normally turn the energy into expecting someone or life to fill it. For example, Gertrude, a client from Germany, is continually upset with her boyfriend because his attention wanders to other women. Her anger doesn't change him and she does not want to leave him either. When she accepts her helplessness in this situation, she contacts a deep feeling of aloneness and isolation that has haunted her all of her life. This is precisely what lies behind her expectations.

Not only do we normally choose not to feel behind our expectations, but often we even deny that we have expectations, needs and wants as a defense against the pain of disappointment, rejection, failure or hurt. We may feel so unworthy that we don't think we deserve anything and this makes our expectations become more deeply buried. When we deny or repress our expectations, they come out indirectly in the form of unexpressed resentments, in chronic depression, in bitchiness, passive aggression or in overt violence.

We cover our expectations with beliefs like:

- "It is not okay to need; we have to learn to take care of ourselves"

- "It is pointless to want or need anything because it won't be met anyway"

- "To express a need only meets with frustration, so why bother"

Our expectations cover a place inside that is deeply wounded and hungry. Looking out from the child's consciousness, the reality that we see in the present is distorted. We project what we experienced long ago onto the present with all the fears and mistrust that we learned from experience. The present may actually be much more safe and loving that we believe, but we can't see it. We still react as a child might.

Without awareness and understanding, it is easy to feel victimized by existence or our lovers for what is happening, instead of seeing that we are the ones who create it. By identifying the pattern with deep compassion and insight, we can begin to alter it. I will explore how this works in much detail later. For now, suffice it to say that the mind of our child has formed beliefs and repeats patterns based on our early childhood experience and we have to find a way to wake up from the movie that is distorting our present reality with projections from our past.

Exercise: Identifying Expectations:

- What are your expectations in the moments when you feel disappointed, frustrated, or deceived?
- What are your expectations when you notice yourself judging something or someone?

- What are your expectations when you notice yourself blaming or complaining about something or someone?
- What are your expectations in sex, communication, being listened to, spending time with someone, food, shelter and the weather?
- Have fun!

******

Chapter 8

Strategies –
The Child State of Consciousness in Action

Our panicked child is devoted to getting what he or she needs. He is very tenacious. This tenacity is hidden behind strategies. Strategies are how we get what we want. We have seen that, in the mind of the child, we have expectations, many of which are unconscious. When we don't get one of these met, we have a choice. We can either feel the pain of not getting it or, as it is usually the case, we move almost instantaneously and unconsciously into a strategy. If we feel the fear or the pain of not getting the need or expectation met, we are not in a strategy. *We move into a strategy in order to avoid feeling fear or pain.*

Demand and Blame (The Hammer)

"Give it to me! I'm sick of your excuses. You're never here for me. What are you in a relationship for anyway if you are never interested in putting any time into it? I want your energy and I want it now." This is the demanding child. When he or she doesn't get what he wants, he gets angry and demands. The energy of entitlement in the hammer says, "I deserve to get it, I want it now and I don't care about your needs or your excuses."

As a child, we throw tantrums, but as an adult we become abusive and violent. The energy of the hammer is aggressive. We use this strategy to overpower and intimidate the other person to get our way. It can be quite irrational, reactive and impetuous. The charge behind the hammer can be very strong because it is fueled with the rage of a child who was abused, ignored, violated, put down or humiliated. And it carries with it the belief that this is the only way to get what we need. Blame is another aspect of this strategy. Behind blame there is a demand that the other person changes. Blame, on one level, feels good. We don't have to feel the pain of not getting what we want and we don't have to take responsibility for our role in the situation. Instead, we can put the

91

responsibility on the other person.

I still have difficulty overcoming my tendency to blame. It seems so right and justified when I am into it! Being a therapist, I can master all the psychological reasons for telling my lover or friend where they are at and how messed up they are. It has taken and still takes much awareness to pull the energy back inside, feel the pain of not getting what I want at that moment and see how I am contributing to the situation. We all blame, but if we do it unconsciously, it destroys intimacy. There is a thin line between learning to express ourselves with passion and blaming. It is so easy to launch into an attack of the other person instead of just expressing pain and frustration. What has helped me is to see where my energy is directed. If it is out and focused on trying to convince or change the other, I am blaming. If it is inside my belly and I am sharing my own experience, even if it involves the other, then the other is less likely to feel blamed or attacked and can listen.

When we use this strategy, it generally causes others to become intimidated or angry and closed. That only increases our panic and the panic of the other and the hammer comes out more strongly. When we use the hammer, we feel some gratification that at least we are not collapsed and can express ourselves forcefully. But as long as this energy is being used not just to express, but also to affect the other person, it is a strategy.

Manipulation (The Hook)

The panicked child in the body of an adult uses all sorts of inventive ways to manipulate. We manipulate with money, with love, with sex, with our intelligence, with our power, with age, with guilt, with love, with giving, with flattering, with pleasing and with dishonesty. We manipulate with pouting, with cutting off and pretending that we don't care or need anything. From a very early age, we learned how to manipulate. We looked at the situation in front of us and calculated how to play with it to get what we wanted. It was a brilliant survival mechanism and one that we all needed. And sometimes our strategies can be subtle and totally unconscious.

Manipulation, as with all the strategies, has a distinctive energy to it. It is deceitful, calculating and dishonest. With the hook, we basically use our intelligence to control another through deceit. Unfortunately, our manipulative behavior becomes unconscious and now we repeat it without knowing. Others see and feel our manipulativeness and pull away to protect themselves. Then we feel more abandoned and afraid and find more reason to be political. Since honesty and straightforwardness did not work as a child, we see no reason to suspect that it would work any better now.

Mina is a powerful and pretty Italian woman in her mid-thirties. She is loving and overbearing. She attracts men who yearn for a mother and then mothers them to death. Of course, she thinks that her nurturing energy is innocent and giving and she doesn't see the manipulativeness behind it. Sam is a rich developer who provides everything for his lover. Of course, Sam's lover is overwhelmed with his generosity and only mildly suspicious that she has become dependent on it. Underneath, she is resentful. Sam thinks that he is just being a loving man.

Guilting (The Feather with a Metal Point)

Guilting is in essence manipulation, but it is so common that it deserves its own section. Many of us have received guilting from an early age, especially if we had a parent who needed us emotionally. Sometimes we get guilted verbally, but most often it is unspoken. It is like a silent prison holding us captive and preventing us from following our own energy or passion for fear of betraying someone we feel responsible toward. Amana and I recently did a session with a couple, which presented a good example of guilting. The man was unhappy in his life and in his work and expected his girlfriend to make him feel better. Because her mother had projected a similar expectation onto her, she felt responsible for his feeling good. He told her that it was a demonstration of her love for him that she "be there for him" when he felt down and because of her past, she bought right into the manipulation. Underneath, she was seething with resentment as we always are when we allow ourselves to be guilted.

Revenge (The Knife)

When someone hurts us, we register the pain. Sometimes we react right away, but often when we have been hurt, we are too shocked, deflated and humiliated to respond. So we store the hurt under our mask that may be pretending that we don't care. Isabella, an Italian client, was telling us that she was still struggling with the fact that her boyfriend had been having an ongoing attraction with a colleague at work. Since nothing had come of it, she was wondering why it still bothered her. Actually, her boyfriend is quite dependent and often behaves like a regressed child with her. Although she has played a good mother for much of their relationship, lately she has been setting limits and pulling way from the mothering role. As an unconscious revenge, he was telling her about this "strong" attraction to this woman at his work.

Inside, we don't rest until we have returned the hurt one way or another, because a wound to our self-respect is the deepest kind of hurt. I never realized the extent to which I was holding resentment inside because I always brushed off my humiliations and pretended that nothing bothered me. But as I delved deeper into this work, I saw that as a child and as an adult, I had accepted so much humiliation that I had become numb to it. Inside, my resentments seethed and leaked out as negative gossip, as judgments or sarcasm. I was too collapsed to express my resentment directly. My favorite revenge tactic has always been to cut off or to become busy. I could do it with a vicious coldness and lack of feeling.

In a state of unconscious relating, revenge has a powerful impact. Unknowingly, we are taking revenge on people for the hurts from the past. A person who triggers our hurt in the present takes the fire for all our buried resentments. We want to hurt the other person for all the hurt we feel inside. It is seldom rational. We can do it directly, through punishing, cutting off, putting the other person down, being sarcastic. We can also do it indirectly by doing something that we know will hurt the other when he or she finds out. Essentially, when we feel hurt, as soon as we recover from the shock and from our collapse, we plan how to settle the score. It can take years, but our wounded child has the memory of an elephant.

Our unconsciousness in relation to our strategies brings us much misery. When we use a strategy, it perpetuates the mistrust that caused us to form the strategy in the first place. The more we use the hammer, or the hook, or the knife, the greater is our belief that this is how we must survive and that it is not safe to open and be vulnerable. People react to our strategies. The mistrust that we carry from childhood creates the very betrayal that we fear. Then our belief that opening and becoming vulnerable leads to betrayal becomes even stronger.

Fixing and Changing (The Screw Driver)

"If you would just listen to me!" "I am not asking for much, but if you could just…" "Why don't you?" and so on. This is the strategy of wanting to fix the other person. And as a therapist with all kinds of insights and perceptions, I am often convinced that I know what is best for someone else, especially Amana. When we are sure that something would be in the best interests of the other person, it is very hard to restrain ourselves. But the motivation is not all holy and altruistic. Behind our best intentions is the desire to change the other person because then we feel more connected, more met, more companionship, more oneness and more potential for even deepening intimacy. Unfortunately, the other person is often not receptive to our suggestions, particularly when he or she feels that we have a hidden agenda.

It takes quite some restraint to contain all our frustration and hopes and to hold back our opinions and our suggestions. But it is important to see that it is a strategy. It is a different story if we feel invited to offer our opinion, or if we ask for permission to make a suggestion. Then it can become very loving. Because I

95

have so much respect for Amana's point of view, I often ask her to tell me what she thinks. And I am learning to do the same (with some difficulty.)

The Blindfold

We have a client whose relationship is falling apart. He and his partner have not communicated or made love for years and they hardly spend any time together anymore. But for him, the relationship is fine. He came to us because his wife is unhappy and convinced him to do a workshop together, but when we asked him if he saw any reason for working on their relationship, he could see no need. For him, the level of their communication is fine because he has never know what it is like to communicate openly and deeply with another and he is so busy in his work as a doctor that he rarely has time free and, naturally, he does not miss what he has never known.

This case is rather extreme but it is not uncommon for us to be in denial of the pain of disconnection when we are in a relationship. It is easier to close our eyes, ears and feelings. My father was like that. He stayed busy, even after he retired, spending the day with his activities. He never learned what it was to be intimate and I would have followed his example had I not learned differently. I can see that I would have turned out just like him. And many of us have been conditioned in denial. That is what we say and learned as a child. It is a very effective strategy. No pain. Safely sheltered in our cave of isolation without knowing what we are missing.

Resignation (The Upside-down Begging Bowl)

When we retreat in despair, on the surface we may believe that we no longer care. We feel the hopelessness and we go into our cave – that familiar, safe, but isolated place inside. We roll the rock in front of the mouth of the cave and feel lonely. Most of us are familiar with this place; it is where we have always gone when the strategies have all failed. I have noticed that hiding in my resignation has always been a deep anger with existence and a wanting things to be different.

Much of our childhood may have been filled with feelings of hopelessness and resignation. It is no surprise to be back here again. But as with the other strategies, this belief becomes a self-fulfilling prophecy. Rather than staying engaged with the other person or life and feeling and expressing our hurt, we cut off and retreat, returning repeatedly to that lonely but safe and familiar inner refuge. Resignation is not a legitimate solution to anything. In truth, it is simply cold anger and resentment.

We cannot live without love. To give up takes us deeply into depression or cynicism. Most of us feel resigned for a while, but because our need for love is so compelling, eventually we come back out of the cave and try again. Then we go until again we discover we are not getting what we want. We try the strategies again, they don't work and we go into the cave. Not a very happy pattern. Yet this is what we all do. How do we get off this vicious and miserable roller coaster? We have to go in and feel the fear and the pain that we are avoiding with our strategies.

The Strategies Have Common Characteristics

Here are some aspects to help identify a strategy:

1) *Each one is a way to affect the other person and to alter his or her behavior so that we get what we want.* In other words, it is a way of trying to change the situation from disappointment to gratification. When we want to get something from someone and we are not aware of this, we will invariably pick up one of these strategies.

2) *Strategies are aspects of our personality and of our layer of protection.* They have nothing to do with our essential nature, but we have become so habituated to them that we mistake them for who we really are.

3) Since it is part of our personality designed to affect others, it can be offensive and *invite negative reaction.* When we then feel

pushed away, we think our being is being rejected and react with strategies. Then we usually get rejected again and this is a very painful downward spiral.

4) The strategies are ways our child learned to behave; to get what he or she wanted. *They are our survival mechanisms.* They are behaviors learned from a past situation but unconsciously applied to the present.

5) To drop out of a strategy, we have to *feel the vulnerability behind it.*

6) *When our strategies work, we hold onto them longer* and it is even more difficult to develop awareness about them.

7) It is extremely difficult to recognize our own strategies. *We have huge blind spots in this area* and are sensitive to receiving feedback about them because we feel attacked.

The Dance of the Strategies

In our relationships, we do "the dance of strategies" much of the time. When one of us feels disappointed, rejected or wanting, rather than express it directly, we usually react with a strategy. Then the other reacts to the strategy with his or her own strategy and the dance is on. It usually ends in conflict, distance and pain.

Robert wants to get up early in the morning to jog and then meditate. He has little time for himself and finds the early morning a special quiet time in the day to be just with himself before going to work. Suzanne wants him to stay in bed and make love. She doesn't see him much and wants this time to connect with him. He wakes up and feels torn, alternating between feeling guilty if he goes and resentful if he stays. She feels his dilemma but wants him to stay. So she tries to seduce him.

He responds at first but then pulls back. Suzanne gets angry and confronts him for never giving her any time. He feels controlled, gets angry, gets up and puts on his jogging clothes without saying anything. Suzanne starts to cry, feeling again deprived and unnourished. Robert refuses to get sucked into guilt and leaves feeling that he can never get the freedom he needs and that no one will ever understand him. Suzanne, left behind and abandoned again, collapses deeper into tears of despair.

Working with the Strategies

Looking at our strategies is a powerful window for looking at ourselves. It is an opportunity to develop an awareness of many unconscious games that we all play that cause us much pain. Bringing consciousness to this deepens our meditation and our ability to have intimacy. *Strategies sabotage intimacy.* Developing some awareness for when and how we use them will increase our ability to become nourished by others. Often when we start bringing more awareness to our strategies, we judge ourselves for what we see. But as scientists exploring our inner world, exploring our unconscious behavior, we have to approach it with much compassion.

It is in the nature of relationships between lovers and friends that we provoke each other. In fact, we tend to be attracted to people who provoke us the most. The other will force us to relive our early experience. Without awareness, it is easy to slip unconsciously into strategies and just keep re-enforcing our old negative beliefs that we have to fight, that we will always be rejected and so on. Each moment is a new opportunity to bring the awareness of the present rather than living in the effects of the past.

Robert in the above example could react automatically, or he could express himself in a new way. Perhaps he could explain how much he needs to spend some time alone and also try to understand Suzanne's feelings. Suzanne, rather than slipping immediately into strategies could listen to Robert, get an understanding for his need and then express her own directly.

Whenever we are in strategy, we are not making a connection with the other person. We may not always know what we are doing, but feeling that pain of not connecting can tip us off that a strategy is in operation. Two hungry reactive children don't connect or nourish each other very well. If we could realize that strategies don't really work, maybe we could stop using them. Unfortunately, that is easier said than done. We use strategies because they cover up a deep seated fear inside that we are not going to get what we want or need. It is a basic mistrust in the benevolence of existence that has arisen out of our wounds of shame, shock and abandonment that I will be exploring later.

Cultivating Inner Space

In my experience, we find the space to feel the pain or fear inside instead of reacting automatically with a strategy when we take the time to go inside. The survival fears we carry are powerful and compelling. But if we begin to take time to go in and feel ourselves again, we develop inner spaciousness. This can come from beginning to take time, even for a few minutes, to stop, close our eyes and go in. When we go in, we may choose to watch our breath, feel the sensations in the body, watch our thoughts, or even to begin to allow ourselves to watch and feel emotions without doing anything. This kind of meditation practice has a way of reconnecting us with the harmony of existence and slowly teaches us to let go and trust again.

Exercise: Identifying your Strategies

Once you become aware of the strategies, you can begin to appreciate how you use them and how they are used on you.

- What are your favorite strategies?
- What do you resort to when you want to get a need fulfilled?
- What do you do when you want something?
- What do you do when you don't get something that you want?
- Investigate the energy behind each of these behaviors.

Part 3

How We Escape From Our Fears

Chapter 9

Confronting Our Delusions About Love

Much of our conditioning is based on avoiding fear and pain. It supports our magical thinking and behavior. As a result, we have constructed a lifestyle built on avoiding these feelings. There is little support in our culture for inner work. It would be hard to imagine walking into a supermarket and hearing a song on the loud speaker about the joys of going inside, of feeling the pain and learning to come out of the child state of consciousness. Instead we would probably hear something like, "My baby just left me and I'm feeling so sad. Why is life always treating me so bad?"

We have been conditioned to run away from ourselves through finding "love". Given the depth of our fear and pain, there is good reason to want to run away from it. One of the greatest deceptions we have is that we will find another person who will make us happy and will take away our fears. We are seldom aware how much our pursuits and dramas of "love" are little more than the child inside of us looking for relief. So, a big part of the journey out of fear is looking at the ways that our love affairs are unconscious and habitual ways of running from our fears.

Facing our Delusions about Love

What is the most common intimate topic that we often share with a friend over a cup of coffee (or herb tea)? Our love stories. They are a major preoccupation. We cannot live without love, but finding it and keeping it is very difficult. Why is it that love which begins with so much hope and promises so often eventually becomes a nightmare? Why is it that love seems so often to deteriorate into a bitter power struggle or cold indifference? And why is it that we repeat the same painful patterns over and over again?

Love is impossible to find and sustain until we have confronted and begun to work with our fear. Until then, our love stories are just a way to try to avoid facing the fear. Here are three ways that, in relation to love and intimacy, we commonly avoid fear:

- We hold onto the belief that we will find someone who will take our fear and pain away, principally the fear of our aloneness

- We delude ourselves into believing that we are self-sufficient, that basically we can make it on our own

- We believe that when pain or fear arises, it is the fault of someone or something outside of ourselves

These are big delusions to overcome. Very big. Much bigger than I ever realized. They have layers of layers of deception to them. We get through one layer only to find there is still another one. The deceptive beliefs and the behaviors that follow them become revealed as soon as we open to another person. Unless exposed and brought into awareness, they will continually sabotage our efforts to find love.

The Romantic Dream

I never realized how deeply addicted and conditioned I was to believing in the romantic dream. I thought that because I was such an "evolved" spiritual seeker this didn't apply to me. I wasn't looking for my princess. But when I started to do co-dependency work, I realized how much I was fooling myself. I just spiritualized it into finding my "soulmate". I don't know if soulmates actually exist, so for me, this concept was just glorified romanticism. I started every new relationship with full expectations that I had finally found the one waiting for me. And for a while, it seemed that way. But eventually when conflict and frustrations arose, the disappointment and disillusionment came.

When we begin to understand about the panicked and traumatized child inside, it is easier to also understand why we would naturally get seduced by fantasies of finding a "perfect partner".

104

In the child's way of thinking and feeling, we can only imagine that the soothing, peace and nourishment we long for must come from the outside.

This fantasy has been seducing us since childhood with enchanting fairy tales. It says, "There is a wonderful prince or princess out there waiting for you and when you find him or her, all your dreams will come true. On a deeper level, what the voice is saying is, "Once you find the right person, your pain and loneliness will be over. This right person will deeply understand and love you, showering you with support, respect and sensitivity."

In another version, one that is just as damaging, the voice says, "As soon as there is conflict, it is time to split. Problems mean that we are not compatible with each other and you are just not with the right person. It is a waste of time and energy to argue, fight, or try to work it out. There is nothing to work out or through; it is time to find someone else. Relationships are not meant be difficult or a struggle." Much of our conditioning is based on perpetuating a myth of the ideal love affair, but in reality, it is just a cover for our reluctance to accept that the "perfect person" is not going to meet all of our needs. We are indoctrinated in this fantasy from childhood through books, love songs, television and movies.

We can sustain the romantic dream during the honeymoon period. Things are fresh enough and we are naive enough that all our projections on the other still hold. They can still get away with being ideal. Furthermore, the fantasy is upheld with a lot of help from our hormones. But when that wears off and time starts to reveal that our lover is not as perfect as we thought, trouble starts. Then we either settle into some co-dependent arrangement or we move on. Surrendering to the romantic dream is easy. But it has nothing to do with surrendering to love. I have learned the hard way that romance has no relation to reality. As long as I held onto the fantasy, I never had to encounter my lack of trust, my fears and my pain of not being loved. I could seek refuge in the idea that someday, someone, somehow... The romantic fantasy shields us from feeling fear because it prevents us from seeing and experiencing life as it is. With it, we project an idea onto life about how we think it should be. We live in hope.

Denial and False Self Reliance

When I looked out while I was growing up, what I saw were people who all seemed highly self-sufficient and self-contained. It was not an environment that supported feeling and expressing feelings. It was many years before I even learned what a need was. The lessons I received taught me that the way to go through life was to develop one's potential, work hard and help others in what you do and do as well as you can. Valuable lessons, but sadly lacking in validating my vulnerability. I learned them well and became highly self sufficient and self contained; a high achiever in total denial of my feminine side. Naturally, when I finally allowed myself to come close to a woman, sooner or later, I would judge her for being too needy and insecure.

This is a highly deceptive way of masking fear because it covered up all the fears that I had about closeness and abandonment. I never even suspected that these fears were inside of me. The voice, which I listened to inside said: "You can take care of yourself. Accept your aloneness because that is how things are. Forget trying to find someone who loves and understands you. It will never happen anyway. You can take care of your own needs much better than anyone else. There really isn't anything that you can't give to yourself and it saves much trouble. If you enter into a love story, you will anyway wind up disappointed and alone again."

I avoided the fear of opening to my needs simply by denying that I had them. I avoided feeling vulnerable or risking being out of control by living in a cocoon of strong self-image, activity, importance, challenges and independence. I discovered later that in co-dependency, there was a name for this kind of person; he is called an "anti-dependent." We buffet this fantasy of self-reliance with addictions – compulsions such as work, alcohol, drugs, sex and so on. To overcome my denial, I had to come out of the

106

trance of pretending that everything was fine and that my needs were being met. What I had was a life robbed of intimacy and depth. Again, when we look at this pattern with an understanding of the panicked child inside, it is easy to see that this could be a natural form of protection from feeling the pain of abandonment. The child, feeling the pain of not being received, appreciated, supported or loved, goes into his or her shell very early and finds a way of surviving that does not rely on others to meet his or her needs.

But the illusion of self-reliance shields us from our fears just as powerfully as does the romantic dream. It does it by hiding us in isolation where we never have to acknowledge or face fear. It isn't until we come out of our isolation and dare to come close to someone that the fears arise. The price we pay for this position is not feeling our vulnerability. And, quite simply, if we can't feel vulnerable we can't have love.

The Consciousness of Blame

With this delusion, it's always the other person's fault and the other person's problem, or it's the environment or the situation that isn't right. In the child state of consciousness, it is natural to blame the outside because we do not feel that we have the resources to get what we need unless we change something or someone on the outside. In that state of consciousness, we cannot feel that we have the ability to give to ourselves what we need. This delusion seems to me to be the hardest one to overcome. I have seen that my blame covered a place inside where I am deeply angry, not even knowing what I am so angry about. Much of it I can trace back to childhood trauma and much of it is just being pissed off with existence for giving me pain and disappointment. Unknowingly, I have projected that anger and hurt on my lovers, on friends, on situations where I felt frustrated and denied. In the heat of disappointment or frustration, it has been almost instinctual for me to move into blame rather than stay with the pain. Why not? It is so much more comfortable to blame rather than feel the pain.

Blaming is quite common. The blame conveniently shifts the energy onto the other person so we don't have to look at ourselves. We all do it. At that moment, it probably doesn't even occur to us that there might be something for us to look at. When someone reminds us to take more responsibility, we agree totally and then add, "But I'm sick of the way she(he) is never there for me and I'm sick of the fact that she (he) never looks at her (his) own stuff." We learn things very quickly intellectually, but when faced with the pain, out comes the blame. It takes a constant awareness to bring the focus back inside and to see that the other person is just a mirror for us to learn more about ourselves. That is no easy pill to swallow.

Of course, giving up blame doesn't mean we don't set limits when we need to. This distinction is one of the most difficult that we deal with in our workshops. Blaming is not the same as setting a limit. When I set a limit, the energy stays with me. I am not throwing it out on the other and making him or her wrong. Setting a limit enhances self-respect and dignity, blame doesn't.

The Decision to Go Inside

These three – romance, self-reliance and blame – are aspects of the child state of consciousness that go very deep into our psyche. These delusions justify us and give meaning to our life. Our romantic notions, our self-reliance or our conviction that the outside causes our pain are some of the pillars that support how we live and understand life. To give them up plunges us into the unknown. Furthermore, we use them unconsciously to stay hidden, protected and safe. Without them, we are naked.

It is terrifying to confront our wounds and few situations provoke them more powerfully than our close relationships. It triggers our feelings of jealousy, abandonment and rejection; our wounds of feeling misunderstood, unloved, or unsupported. But I am convinced from my own life that once we turn the energy inside and sincerely begin to look at ourselves, transformation happens. We don't even need to worry about digging up buried childhood or past life memories. Our current life and especially, our significant relationships bring up all the patterns, all the wounds and all the material that we need to work with.

******

Chapter 10

The Drama of the Dependent and the Anti-Dependent

One of the most powerful ways that we avoid contacting our fear and pain inside is to get lost in endless relationship dramas, repeating the same patterns over and over again. Until we discover what lies underneath these dramas, our life is filled with continual disappointment and frustration. Let's look at the drama. At its core, it is the drama of the *dependent* and the *anti-dependent.*

Setting the Stage

This drama doesn't begin until the honeymoon period is over. The honeymoon is an altered state, like a drug. We are lost in fantasy, in positive projections that haven't yet been damaged with time and familiarity. We feel open and overflowing with love. Each new person becomes the container for all the positive projections we have about the ideal lover. For a while, for as long as the dream lasts, we can hold the projection. Generally during this stage, there may be little or no conflict. Sex is great and the compatibility seems next to perfect. Our defenses go down and we enjoy a period of wonderful melting and merging, something we all deeply hunger for. Our energy expands with this new aliveness. We project on our lover many needs that were unmet in childhood and during this period, we actually believe that the needs will be met.

Sooner or later, the energy begins to change, sometimes in a crash landing, sometimes in a lingering period of disillusionment. We have allowed someone to come close, past a certain limit that we normally and often unconsciously keep up in relation to others. This person has opened our doors – at least temporarily. But once open, we are also more open to disappointment. We came out of our isolation and have opened to love. When we open, we also open to our trauma – the trauma of abandonment and invasion.

111

And trauma without awareness leads to co-dependency. The honeymoon's end can crash into us as a crushing feeling of disappointment and despair. We realize that our deepest expectations for fulfillment may actually not be met, that this person just isn't the ideal soul mate we thought he or she was. We have gone from the dreamland of positive projections to the nightmare of negative projections. Then what often happens is that we polarize into one of two positions, two emotional stances. One person wants more love, togetherness, attention and connection while the other person craves more alone time, more space and more freedom. It is the drama of the "Dependent" and the "Anti-Dependent."

The Anti-Dependent Meets the Dependent

A couple who recently did one of our workshops offers a good example of a situation that seems to be almost universal. John and Cathy have been lovers and living together for over four years. For the first years of their relationship, they both enjoyed a wonderful honeymoon period, without conflict, appreciating each other and feeling that they had found their soul mates. However, in the past year, things have become strained between them. Their differences in priorities have become more exaggerated and they are fighting more often.

Both are feeling frustrated and beginning to suspect that something is very wrong. John prizes his freedom, independence and his spiritual search above everything and is feeling pressured by Cathy. Cathy, who values intimacy and taking the time to go deep with her lover, is feeling that she never has the time with John that she wants and that he is seldom emotionally available.

Here is an excerpt from one of their interactions:

Cathy: "I can't stand it when you cut off from me. You spend so much time doing all your little things, because you're so afraid of letting someone get close to you."

John: "I wouldn't have any trouble getting close to you if you would stop being so needy. I can't stand the way you always harp on closeness and sharing. It drives me nuts."

Cathy: "It drives you nuts because you are so terrified that if you let someone get close to you, you wouldn't be so much in control all the time."

John: "Bullshit! You are just as interested in control. You want to control me so that I am just how you want me to be. You're so afraid of being alone that you just want to hide in relationship. That isn't intimacy; it's addiction."

Cathy: "Oh, and the way you are so obsessed with work all the time and all your little activities; that's not an addiction?"

John: "Okay, I think that we both have something to look at. But there is no way that any of this can be worked out unless you meditate more."

Cathy: "Your meditation trip is just another escape. What we need is to make love more, not meditate more."

And on it goes. Sound familiar?

The Anti-Dependent

The anti-dependent avoids intimacy because he (or she) has felt betrayed by "love". What he experienced in the name of love was often manipulation, possessiveness, engulfment, over-protection or feeling needed to fill the emotional needs of his (or her) parent. Therefore, in his current relationship, he attracts love because he needs it but then rejects it when it gets too close or when he senses the slightest demand on his "freedom", which he has cultivated so well.

I know the role of the anti-dependent well because I played it perfectly in my former intimate relationships. I was almost phobic of having someone come too close for fear of being smothered. All the women I had been with in long-term relationships had similar complaints. They admired and were attracted to my intelligence, self-reliance, dedication and commitment with whatever I did, my devotion to the spiritual search and my caring. But they found me too structured and rigid, emotionally unavailable and always felt low on my priority list.

I was not available emotionally to others because I was not available emotionally to myself. Because of so much shock, it has always been so difficult to access my feelings and even more difficult to share them. Because there is so much distrust of being genuinely seen and loved, I have been very protected and guarded emotionally. I wanted desperately to open to a woman, but there has always been a deep mistrust that it will mean giving up my freedom and compromising my spiritual intensity for the sake of romance. I have always distrusted all the emotional "trips" that seem to go along with relationships and have hated the thought of being weighted down with a lot of drama. Yet the alternative, living alone, has also seemed dry and unnourishing. So, I kept trying, but each time running into the same barriers. At a certain point, I felt pulled on and started to retreat, going back into my safe inner refuge that I knew so well. My partners reacted in anger and frustration and I responded by pulling back even further, feeling more suffocated and indignant.

I yearned for truth in relating, but when I looked out from my isolation at the women who wanted to share their heart with me, what I saw was mostly emotional dependence, control and manipulation. If I opened, I felt that I would be totally dominated. This situation was pure anguish. My heart was closed and I didn't know what to do with the hungry and mistrusting child inside. It was like a prison of my own making without a door to get out. Obviously, all of this had something to do with my mothering. My mother was over-protective, shielding me from my fears (and hers also). On some level, I must have also wanted it, but as a result, I lost myself. To come close to a woman again brought up the same fear of being controlled or dominated. But my deepest fear in coming close to a woman was really the fear of taking on and becoming fused with her fears. I covered that with the rap that I was being diverted from my spirituality and my creativity. To deal with these fears that I was projecting, I had to open to my own fears.

My anti-dependency also had something to do with the model of intimacy that I got from my father. A deeply sensitive man, he expressed his soul through playing classical music and working with people. (He spent most of his working life helping displaced Jewish refugees all over the world.) But he lacked the tools or awareness to share his fears and vulnerability with others. As a result, I learned also to isolate myself and hide my feelings. Only when I started to acknowledge the depth of my own fears did I begin to change my pattern. As an anti-dependent, I was simply acting out of the fears rather than facing them. It has become clearer that the fears were based on past reality and I was continually recreating these in the present. Learning to set limits and to risk coming out of my old patterns of withdrawing has helped me to go into the fears of intimacy.

And now, surprisingly enough, I am experiencing the other side of the coin – what it is like to feel dependent. In our work, when we move from the anti-dependent to the dependent, we call it "crossing the first river". Not so long ago, I got a call from an acquaintance who also leads workshops. Earlier, he was leading awareness workshops which were a bit disconnected emotionally. But now, after being in a relationship for a year, he has begun to work with intimacy and relating in his workshops. He told me that since falling so deeply in love with the woman he is with now, for the first time in his life, he is feeling what it is like to be dependent on someone, to have fears coming up of needing her, of losing her, of feeling jealous and insecure.

The Dependent

The dependent clings because he or she is desperate for love. There is a profound wound of abandonment that comes out as a panic to hold onto the other. This clinging, or obsessive jealousy or hyper-vigilance that the other is not really there covers a severe panic of being left and of being alone. The dependent behavior is a way of escaping from *feeling and pain;* the fears of abandonment.

A friend, Allison, has been with her lover for over ten years. She is deeply in love with him, but even after all this time, is just learning how not to be afraid of him; afraid of his anger and his rejection. When around him, she can easily lose herself. She often finds it difficult to feel herself or to communicate what she is feeling. This is particularly strong whenever he is critical of her. Her fears of rejection are so overwhelming, she cannot bear the thought of him leaving her and because of that, much of her life revolves around his needs and wants. Alone or with friends, it is easier for her to be confident and with herself. Although she has had many other lovers in the past and still attracts the attention of other men, she finds that she has little trust that if she lost her lover that she would ever find anyone like him again; so sensitive, strong and so committed to the truth and to his growth.

In fact, by now, she has no idea of what it would be like to be without him. Just the thought of it has terrified her. Gradually, by doing this work so intensively, she is beginning to find the courage to give herself the space that she needs. It has been a slow process learning to trust herself and to find the courage to do and say what she needs to without being so terrified of rejection or anger.

The Anti-Dependent in Relationship

Walk into an anti-dependent's room and you may find it looking like a Zen temple; sparse, essential and neat. In one corner, a miniature library of Zen literature, in another corner a statue of Buddha sitting in deep, beatific meditation and in front of it, a meditation cushion with Tibetan bells on top. All very neat, silent and undisturbed. (I speak from experience.) Or, the room might look like a storage place for outdoor sports equipment; wind surfing gear, rock climbing paraphernalia, tennis rackets and swimming goggles.

Aloneness, freedom, solitude and meditation are his (or her) gods. And he rationalizes his position by setting up a belief system that maintains that going into aloneness is what life is about. Naturally, he will find all the right literature to support this position. "Look at this passage about aloneness," he might say to his lover, hoping that each new passage will finally convince her of the truth of his point of view. But all these gods are actually false gods because his aloneness, freedom and meditation are covering up a deep need to be touched and a deep need for warmth and affection. We can be highly disciplined, but the discipline is usually a compensation for deep underlying emptiness and insecurity.

True, an anti-dependent may have some understanding for independence and freedom. His (I use "he" but an anti-dependent can just as easily be a "she") search for a state of detachment is sincere, but it is incomplete because his heart is closed. He may have learned how to spend long periods of time alone, but there is deep pain in this aloneness. The freedom he searches for can only come if it includes love. But he is so afraid of love that he constructs rigid beliefs that cover up a deep terror for becoming dependent and losing control. He doesn't see his own power games. In his "self-sufficiency", he can easily shame and abuse his lover because he is not in touch with his own woundedness. And rather than feel his own pain, he puts his energy into blame and abuse. If he fears that his lover may leave, he may make a gesture of opening, but it is just a game. Once he is back in control, the old behavior begins again.

To relieve all the tension and pain from continually covering up the underlying need for emotional contact, he may seek relief with alcohol or drugs or compulsive work. But that makes him even more cut off from himself and the downward spiral continues, often becoming more and more self-destructive. Finally his lover begins to see that all efforts to establish lasting emotional contact are hopeless. He or she may get in occasionally, but then is pushed away over and over again and finally leaves in exasperation. At this point, the anti-dependent may come to his knees. He may actually come face to face with

117

his deep loneliness if he can allow himself to feel the pain, recognize that he is repeating a painful pattern and start looking inside. But usually, he just blames the other for being too needy, or finds some other excuse for the failure of the relationship, furthering his conviction that love is impossible. He loses himself in some distraction until the next time he "falls in love". Then the movie starts all over again. He finds himself facing a new person, hearing the same feedback and saying in bewilderment, "Gee, haven't I heard that before somewhere?"

The Dependent in Relationship

The dependent's room is no Zen temple. On the contrary, it is more often a Tantric temple; soft lighting, pillows, flowers, aroma lamps and Indian Karma sutra pictures. While the anti-dependent lectures on aloneness, freedom, and independence, the dependent has an excellent rap on sharing, intimacy and openness. It is war; Zen vs. Tantra. Like the anti-dependent, the dependent also has false gods. What he or she calls intimacy and love is not real because it arises out of fear. The dependent's fear of aloneness can be just as sabotaging to relationship as the anti-dependent's fears of intimacy. If these fears are avoided, the dependent is forever in search of someone who will shelter him or her from his fears. What happens is that the other person or life will continually force him back on himself through being deprived or rejected.

The dependent's fear, or actually terror, is of being alone and of being unloved. His or her efforts to get love are often desperate. He or she becomes a pleaser, a complier and a beggar, leaning toward the other to get love; waiting, hoping and frustrated. He or she is looking for that someone who is really willing to open, who is committed to the relationship and who doesn't put the intimacy at the end of his list of priorities. When alone, he or she suffers, but when with another, he or she waits for whatever crumbs of affection he or she can get. Once in relationship, it is almost impossible to let go because so much of his or her identity, well-being and sense of self is wrapped up in the other. Dependents have poor boundaries and are always getting lost in the other.

Her emotional expression, while intense and total, can often be a way of avoiding feeling rather than being with it. Because the anti-dependent often feels some guilt for his lack of presence and feeling, the dependent can use feelings as a way of manipulating her lover. Often when the dependent claims to be coming from a place of vulnerability and openness, it is a "power trip", full of expectation, demand and desire to control the other. Naturally, this produces a reaction and instead of love, we have World War III. The dependent's desire for intimacy is always contaminated with needs for which she is not taking responsibility. Her efforts to get intimacy are tainted with a subtle manipulation, accusing the other of not wanting to open. It creates guilt that only leads to more distance and conflict.

The Drama Can Be the Stimulus to Take Us Inside

What makes the drama so interesting and so difficult to escape from is that in either case, we are convinced that we are right. And in a way we are – half right. We can see the hypocrisy and falsehood in the other, but unfortunately not in ourselves. Many of my co-dependency counseling sessions begin with either person complaining about the other. Usually dependents book groups and sessions more often than anti-dependents because they are more invested in the relationship working, while anti-dependents deal with the disharmony by meditating, mountain climbing or working.

Also, as a dependent, we are generally more in touch with our pain. To end the drama we have to look inside instead of focusing on the other. Sooner or later, after enough repetitions, we start to see that while the characters may change, the drama continues. In fact, this drama is often what forces us to go in. Anti-dependents and dependents will find each other. They are two parts struggling to become whole and each has projected the missing part on the other. These two types must find each other in order to recognize the part of them that is missing. That is what produces the energy of attraction. When the courting game takes

119

place, the energy between us is not only biological, it is also the higher consciousness in both of us seeking an opportunity to become whole. Unfortunately, we often lack the awareness and understanding to use the situation to go in and learn more about ourselves. Instead, we get lost in the drama.

The healing is not complicated. The Dependent needs to learn to contain the frustration of not getting what he or she wants by feeling the pain and fear that comes up and also express needs without expectation. The Anti-Dependent needs to risk to open again in intimacy and also take whatever space he or she needs for aloneness without asking for permission.

Feeling Despair is a Good Starting Point

It is easy to reach a point of feeling hopeless about ever working it out, about ever finding love in our life. But from my experience that is a good point to reach. It gives us enough motivation to do the inner work we need to do. These patterns will not resolve themselves simply by looking at the problems of the relationship or by questioning our compatibility with our lover or by being convinced that it's the other's problem. We are not going to work it "out", we have to work it "in". We won't resolve this mess without getting to the root. We have both an anti-dependent and a dependent inside of us. We may discover that in different relationships or in the same one. *But sooner or later, we have to go into both our fears of aloneness and our fears of intimacy.*

Exercises: Exploring the Dependent and Anti-Dependent

Take a moment to investigate your own pattern in relationships. In those relationships where you were the most deeply affected, do you notice that you are predominately dependent or anti-dependent?

Perhaps you see that you have been both. Choosing the last significant relationship, which one did you play? If you are not sure, then pick one while we investigate together what it feels like inside.

The Anti-Dependent

If you found that you took an anti-dependent position, allow yourself to tune into the ways that you protect yourself from someone getting too close. Recognize, without judgment, that if you are protecting, there is a deep and valid fear underneath. Imagine that you are putting up a shield and using this shield to keep a distance from the person you are or have been close with. Feel the energy of the shield. Then feel the person who is behind the shield. What is he or she protecting against?

Consider the following questions and see if they apply to you:

- Are you afraid that you will lose yourself in the other? That you won't know what you want anymore, or won't be able to feel yourself?

- Are you afraid that your heart will be taken advantage of? Afraid that if you open your heart, the other person will drag you down with his or her pain? Afraid that you have to take care of her or him?

- Do you feel that you need space; space to find yourself, not to be demanded of, space to explore your creativity and your silence? Are you afraid that you will be smothered, that you won't be able to breathe if you let someone in?

- Do you feel irritation and anger when you feel the other person's expectations and anger at not wanting to live up to their demands and expectations? Is there anger that the other person is not willing to take responsibility for their own pain?

- Do you feel, at a deep level, that you will never be understood and that if you open, you will be abused, manipulated, or rejected? Feeling the little boy or girl inside, can you connect with a deep mistrust? Is your child inside hungry for love and acceptance, but afraid that he or she will be betrayed and abused?

The Dependent

Exploring the dependent position, imagine that you are in a begging posture. Imagine that you have a begging bowl in your hands and you are reaching out for love. Let yourself feel the waiting and the hoping that you will get the love that you are waiting for

Consider the following questions:

- Are you waiting for the right person to come along, someone who is sensitive enough to love you and open? Or do you start feeling a hopelessness or sadness that you will never get it?

- Do you see yourself giving away your dignity and your power to the other person, afraid of being rejected, or shamed and abused? Do you feel a panic of losing the other person's love?

- Do you feel a frustration of never getting what you want, an anger of being cut off over and over again, opening and then feeling your lover pull away over and over again? Is there an anger for all the ways that the other person hooks you in, but is actually never willing to be there, really there?

- Is there a feeling that you are basically not worthy of love? Not worthy of being loved in a way that will really allow you to relax and be nourished?

Chapter 11

Compensations -
Roles and Behaviors We Use to Avoid Feeling Fear

Compensations are about control. They cover our fear. They are the ways that we hide our fear and our shame from ourselves and others. They are the habitual and unconscious roles and behaviors that protect us from threat or from feeling pain. It was essential for our survival and sanity that we could find ways to bear the assaults and traumas that we sustained as a child. Our compensations were basically the ways we dealt with all the aggressive and insensitive energies that invaded us. We learned to please or to withdraw or to fight or to try and control this offensive energy in whatever way we could. We learned these behaviors from what we saw others doing.

We learned our compensations to protect ourselves, but these compensations also made us lose touch with ourselves because they took us away from our nature and our essence. Whenever we are in a compensation, our essential energy is compromised, we are not real and we are playing a role to stay safe. Generally we don't know that. We don't know what is real or what is a compensation until we experience the real again, until we come home to ourselves again.

I learned very early to please and perform in the ways that were expected of me. And it wasn't until much later that I even realized that who and how I was acting wasn't me. Something always felt wrong, but I had no idea what it was. I had nothing to compare with. I had no idea who the real me was. My conditioning taught me that my self-worth was based on what I accomplished and what I did, not on who I was. So, I put my energy into achieving and pleasing and a deeper part of me was always hidden and removed.

Our compensation can get penetrated in moments when something out of the ordinary happens to us, when existence in some way shatters our control. And in these moments, perhaps when we lose a loved one, or when we suffer a serious rejection in love or in our work, we may wake up. I am not quite sure what finally helped me begin to discover my real self, but at a certain point, I started realizing the difference between what felt real and what felt false. Then slowly my life started to change very drastically. The more willing we are to allow this process to happen, the less dramatic will be the methods that existence has to use to help us come back to our real self.

The Roots of Compensation

One of the most important factors that helped me to penetrate my compensations was to understand where they came from. Compensations can give us energy, attention, control, identity and power. We compensate in countless ways, with countless roles and behaviors, but at the *root of all of our compensations is fear.* We please in an attempt to harmonize our environment so it becomes safe, we fight in order to feel some mastery over our environment, we withdraw to get distance from the threat we perceive in the environment and we mentalize and analyze to make some sense of the chaos in our environment. We keep busy so we never have to stop and feel our fear. We makes rules for ourselves and others to create safety, conformity and homogeneity. We use power, money or sex to control others and we therapize, teach or preach to control our world.

The fears behind all this endless exhausting behavior are that:

- We will have to face the fear that we cannot control the events of our life

- We will have to face the shame that deep inside we feel worthless

- We will have to face the pain of rejection and abandonment

- We will have to face the fear of invasion, insensitivity and disrespect

124

Let's explore some of our major compensations in more depth. As I describe each style, take a moment to consider how you may have used this form of protection to keep your vulnerable child safe.

1) Pleasing/Harmonizing

In this style, *we attempt to soften and soothe the threatening energy outside.* Many of us were raised in an environment that was highly male and rational and the pressure and repressed anger inherent in that kind of atmosphere put us in shock. We try to deal with the anxiety by trying to soften the abusive energy. We please in order to avoid having to confront someone or receiving anger. Our efforts to harmonize also express beautiful and natural qualities of wanting to generate love and harmony, but the price we pay for giving our power away over and over again is very high.

Being a pleaser is shaming. It takes a heavy toll on our dignity and self-respect. I never realized until I began to work on my own shame and humiliation, how collapsed and unempowered I was. Becoming a pleaser was a big part of my survival, but it left me feeling castrated and shamed inside. I had become so identified with this role that I didn't see that it wasn't really me. Plus, I bolstered my self-esteem by thinking that I was such a nice person. We can deceive ourselves into thinking that our sweetness is spiritual, nonviolent and loving, without recognizing the degradation that usually goes with this behavior and the mountains of resentment we are hiding underneath.

2) Controlling/Caretaking

In this role, *we cover our fear by trying to control our environment any way we can by trying to control and dominate it.* Rather than become intimidated with the dangerous energy, we move out to overpower or control it. We control in many ways. One very common form is parenting; having someone to need us and become dependent on us. Another is tyrannizing; using our power to overwhelm others through violence or the threat of

125

violence, through words, money, sex and intellect – anything that works. I can see my tyrant in my righteousness, rigidity, judgmentalness, discipline and ambition, placing on myself and on others the same high standards that were placed on me.

The resentment we store by pleasing, we act out and give back to others by controlling and tyranizing as soon as we can. I remember as a medical intern being shocked both in myself and in my fellow neophyte doctors at how quickly we learned to abuse those underneath us – the medical students, the nurses, the staff and especially the patients. As medical students, we were often humiliated by interns and residents. Now was our chance to get even. The hurts from all the humiliations in our past get registered and are somehow just waiting for an opportunity to be avenged. We act out the same dynamic in our intimate relationships. Because of repressed hurts, insults and injuries, the controller acts out natural leadership and caring qualities in a distorted way.

3) Mentalizing and Analyzing

Another common way that we compensate is by becoming mental. The energy moves out of our body into our head so we feel safe, secure and in control. We put experience in boxes so that life doesn't seem too overwhelming. We think that we know, but actually it is blocking us where from any true knowing. I never realized how vicious this kind of protection can be. The cynicism and sarcasm that often accompanies the intellectual defense can be deadly. We wall off what is incomprehensible and frightening and reject it, often becoming violent in our righteousness. We are covering up tremendous fear and repressed anger in the tension to make things fit our mental constructs. I know it well. It is one of the main ways that I learned to protect. I witnessed it being used by both my parents and, actually, I think that it is the most characteristic defense of Jewish conditioning.

In the ashram in India where I lived for many years, there was a program for new arrivals. Often people started with therapy groups and then worked in some capacity in the community. The

126

specific groups and work projects recommended were designed to give people what was most needed for their emotional and spiritual growth. When I first got there twenty five years ago, I was full of all kinds of spiritual and psychological ideas about how to direct my growth. But the groups and work projects suggested for me were all focused at getting me out of my head. I was not aware how mental I was, but to others, it was obvious. I spent four years doing manual jobs – carpentry, cleaning, construction – completely divorced from anything I had done in the past, such as therapy or medicine. Some of the time, I resisted and bitched, but somewhere, I knew it was perfect. Now, I am incredibly grateful for the experience, although I would not have created it on my own.

4) Fighting/Rebelling

The fighter/rebel inside expresses the rage of our wounded child by moving out to challenge any threat of invasion or abuse. It says "No!" Our rebel gives us the courage to break the bonds of our conditioning, to detect the pretension, denial and delusion that surrounds us and to break out and destroy all that is mundane, polite and conventional.

But in fighting and rebelling, our anger is unconscious. *We get lost in reaction, attacking and defending, continually suspicious and guarded, always wary of being abused and misunderstood. We become impetuous and jump to conclusions often without taking the time to see or feel where the other person is coming from. Anger and reaction become our way of not feeling our pain,* fear and helplessness or the grief and sorrow in our soul. The fighter can be addicted to adversity. With a kind of righteous arrogance, the rebel becomes identified with his negativity. Everything is a fight and he lives with a chip on his shoulder anticipating and even creating conflict.

The healthy aspect of this compensation style is that we may be more connected with the life energy and passion inside and start to live it. We have come out of collapse, but until we clean up the reactiveness and the paranoia of the fighter, it is still an unconscious part of our protection and one that brings us much isolation and pain.

5) Withdrawing/Going In

One of the easiest ways of protecting ourselves is simply to space out and retreat into our own world, *pulling our energy away from the threatening object or from a world that seems overwhelming, noisy, insensitive and too fast.* I recognize this place as a deeply hidden inner refuge that has been more or less a part of me as long as I can remember. In fact, this was and still is my deepest survival place. I call it my cave. I shut down and went away a long time ago and learned to nourish myself alone. I can see that each time I open, I am actually coming out of my cave where I am alone and comfortably doing my own thing.

When I first began to recognize this, I noticed that with the slightest disappointment, I would retreat back into my cave. My lovers would get frustrated and enraged by my continual withdrawing whenever something heated or uncomfortable came up. But once threatened, I was virtually unreachable. Many of us probably experience that to relate intimately requires coming out from a place that is completely withdrawn and terrified to open. There is some power and fulfillment in the aloneness, but it is not nourishing.

Our withdrawer carries a strong feeling of resignation and hopelessness that can be almost impenetrable. Our withdrawing is very closely connected to the tremendous grief that we are holding inside. But to feel the pain, we have to let go of the security of our aloneness or the resignation and hopelessness. As long as our withdrawing compensation remains unconscious, it keeps us insulated from our feelings. We space out, become confused, retreat into fantasies, regress into an irresponsible child and remain disconnected from ourselves.

We call withdrawal the poet's protection because it protects the poet inside each of us, the one who is highly sensitive, solitary and introspective. The positive aspect of this protection is that the tremendous amount of energy that might otherwise be spent in trying to harmonize, fight or control can be used instead for creativity and introspection. But withdrawers are also often extremely emotionally impoverished without knowing it and harbor unconscious anger for past insults to his dignity.

Identifying Our Negative Movie

Our compensations are not only unconscious habitual patterns of protection, but also they form a belief system based on our deprivation of love and support in childhood. This belief system is like a movie that is running in our head determining how we see and feel the world around us. For instance, when we are pleasing, we believe that it is not safe to be direct and assertive. If we are controlling, we believe that unless we control, something terrifying will happen. When we are fighting, we believe that it is either fight or be controlled. When we withdraw, we believe that the world is just too insensitive a place to stick around in. When we are running this movie, we don't see life around us as it really is; we see it through the perspective of a wounded child. The patterns and the beliefs we formed about life developed out of those original impressions. In our unconsciousness and to the mind of our wounded child, we still see the world as it was to our child. These beliefs anchor us in a delusional but negative and familiar way.

An event in the present can set off a chain reaction inside, which starts the movie and seems to validate the negative beliefs of the movie. For instance, someone says something to us that we interpret as a put down. Immediately, our guard goes up and we feel distrustful. The statement whether true or not has started the movie to run because it has triggered a place inside that remembers having our innocence and trust betrayed. We now perceive that person as the enemy. The movie says, "I'd better watch out. If I open, I will be hurt." Or, "I have to take care of myself because there is no one looking out for me and the world is not a friendly place." Or, "If I don't take what I need, I'll never get what I need." Or, "People are generally interested in repressing my creativity and my life energies, so I have to go for

129

what I want" and so on. Once the movie starts, it is hard to get it to stop and sometimes it runs for much longer than two hours.

Naturally, in our intimate relationships, these beliefs get provoked and set our protective mechanisms into action all the time. It's like having our own emotional computer keyboard where each key triggers a different negative belief. Our lover and close friends play at this keyboard all the time. They push a button and we are gone, shut down, protected and withdrawn, on the attack and the defensive. It takes a great deal of awareness to realize that what we see is not what is, especially when it is someone close to us. It is also not easy to see that our beliefs actually create someone doing exactly what we believe they will do. Most of the time, our protective behavior has become obsolete and we use our protection, even though it is often unneeded.

The Pain of Compensation Brings Us Out

Usually, *what brings us out of our automatic compensation mechanisms is that they hurt.* These roles are isolating and cut us off from our heart, from others' hearts and from our deeper self. Pleasing is humiliating, controlling pushes people away, living life in a constant fight is isolating and damaging to our heart, mentalizing cuts us off from our life energy and withdrawing eventually leads to deep despair, depression, or cynicism. When we live in our compensations we are oriented toward the outside and we are cut off from ourselves, from finding out our true beauty. Unfortunately, it is rare that we drop these patterns without existence coming along and giving us a mighty Zen stick, such as a lover leaving us, or our having an accident or illness.

We adopted all of these protective styles to give space and love to ourselves in an atmosphere where we felt frightened, unloved and unseen. We developed them so that we did not have to feel the intolerable pain of our childhood. When we begin to connect with the fear and the pain, the compensations slowly and naturally melt away.

130

Bringing Awareness to Our Compensations

We can begin to bring awareness to our compensations by beginning to notice when we are in them and feeling the fear behind them in a way that is loving and nonjudgmental. We can get to know them by watching them in action and becoming familiar with how each one feels inside. When we are pleasing, it has a certain feeling in the body that we can learn to recognize. So does withdrawing, controlling and fighting. Becoming sensitive to the body feeling of these roles is, in my experience, the best way to identify them. We can also watch our compensations at work in all of our significant relationships. If we are at a loss, all we have to do is ask our lover or close friends. They'll know. These are the ways we keep a distance, the ways that we protect, the ways that we play power games with each other. It takes some unraveling to uncover them and quite some courage to let go of them. But we can start by recognizing them and sharing them as they arise.

Working to unravel our protection and compensations takes some commitment and compassion. In some ways, it doesn't get easier, it gets harder because our defenses and protections just become more and more subtle. The unwillingness to penetrate our compensations and feel the fear and pain underneath is also the place where most intimate relationships crumble. One or both are not willing to "look at their stuff". If we are gently committed to looking at our blind spots, we can invite those close to us to show them to us. We let them in.

Exercises and Meditations: Identifying the Pleaser and the Tyrant

Identify a main person in your life who in some way frightens you. Perhaps they have power over you in one way on another, or they make you feel inferior, weak and inadequate. Now, imagine that one of them is sitting in front of you and ask yourself the following questions:

- How do you feel sitting in front of him or her?

- How do you feel in your body?

- How do you feel about yourself?

- What happens to your energy?

- How do you relate to him or her?

- Do you judge yourself and try to change yourself?

Now identify a main person in your life with whom you feel in some way superior. Again, imagine that you are sitting in front of them and ask yourself the same questions.

Meditation: How We Learned to Compensate

You can do this exercise as a guided meditation by having a friend read it to you. Close your eyes and allow yourself gently to go inside. Tune into your breath, gently watching the inhale and the exhale. Allow yourself to relax and gently settle into your breath, relaxing with it and allowing it to take you inside. Slowly and gently, going deeper and deeper, more and more relaxed.

Now, imagine that you are inside a cave. This cave is your protected and safe space. In the cave, you are safe but isolated and alone. No one can come inside. You have found ways to be creative in your cave. Perhaps you write, or draw, or play music, whatever you like to do. See yourself in your own cave. What does it look like, how does it feel? Look all around. What have you put in your cave?

Now imagine that you go to the entrance of the cave and you look out. You are looking out at the world outside your cave. What do you see? Is there anyone there? Does it feel safe to come out?

Now imagine that there is someone outside and for some reason, you are drawn to this person. Gently and cautiously, you come out. You come out expecting that you will be greeted with love and warmth. You would like to be seen and appreciated. You are young, innocent, and unsure of yourself. You would like that this person gives you some recognition and approval. Instead, the energy that you encounter is harsh, judging and hurtful. Perhaps this person speaks to you in way that puts you down or humiliates you. Perhaps you are just ignored. Perhaps the person is too busy and just has no time for you. Perhaps, he or she is telling you what he wants and expects from you.

Allow yourself to feel what happens inside. How do you feel the hurt? Does it shock you? Does it anger you? And how do you react to this person. Do you try to soften the person's energy, wanting to make friends and get love? Do you try to please this person? Do you collapse under the harshness or the anger that you feel coming at you? Do you pull back into yourself far away from this offending energy? Do you fight, enraged by the disappointment and betrayal? Spend a moment considering these different responses.

Now imagine leaving the person or people and returning to your cave. How does it feel? Does it feel different from before? Would you like to go back out? Perhaps you are not sure which you prefer? Stay with this feeling for a while. Now, take a deep breath and slowly allow yourself to come back.

******

Chapter 12

Addiction –
Habitual Patterns of Protection

My understanding of addiction used to be very one-dimensional. Before doing this work, it never occurred to me that much of my behavior was grounded in avoidance of deeper feelings of fear and pain. I recognized substance abuse as an obvious addiction, but looking closer, I began to see that much of the behavior that we commonly consider as normal can actually be a subtle form of addiction. I can see that much of our socializing, eating sweets, judging others and analyzing, for example, are rooted in avoidance of looking deeper; ways that we fill our time and head so that we can avoid feeling. With this work, I began to become more sensitive to the ways that I dilute my intensity and the ways that I leak my energy with distraction. Awareness of the wounds buried inside and how difficult it is to access them has changed my understanding of much of my lifestyle.

We all have our addictions, sometimes we are aware of them, and sometimes we aren't. To take a journey deep inside sooner or later we have to investigate and befriend what we do habitually to avoid feeling what is arising for us in the moment and more precisely, to avoid feeling fear and pain. I can see that addiction is a choice that I make, consciously or unconsciously, to become unaware, not to be present in the moment. In terms of the model that I have presented, we are unconsciously drawn to addiction to avoid entering into the layer of vulnerability. Even on a deeper level, we use addiction in its many forms to avoid feeling the emptiness that we all have to face eventually. Viewed in the light of the path of meditation and truth, it isn't just feeling fear and pain that we avoid, it is feeling the empty hole inside that is the gap between mind and no-mind.

Addiction is a distraction from the fear of feeling this emptiness. Much has been written about addiction and co-dependency. In fact, the co-dependency work arose out of inquiring into the

135

reason people abused substances. My focus here is to look at what role it plays in our journey inside and its relation to meditation and how to use meditation to heal addiction. Addiction is part of our protective layer because it effectively impedes our entering into our middle layer. In fact, it operates right at the boundary between the outer and middle layer, between protection and feeling. It acts as an energetic barrier to prevent the fears and pain from arising to the surface from our unconscious.

From my experience, it's not so much the pain but the fear of facing the wounds and the emptiness inside that causes us to try to avoid. It is the fear that we have to encounter and go through. It is the fear of letting go of control. We keep our life in a permanent state of semi-addiction just to avoid having to face the fear. It is often startling for our participants when we suggest that such common habits as smoking cigarettes, excessively drinking coffee or eating sweets is unconsciously motivated by fears of facing our feelings of deprivation, unworthiness or emptiness. The connection between the behavior and the feelings we are blocking is not so obvious because it has become familiar and habitual. Our addictive habits have become a chronic smoke screen between our conscious and unconscious minds.

But even if we try to avoid feeling, life has a way of driving us into our feeling layer anyway. If we resist what life wants to teach us, the lessons come very painfully. When a close friend of mine nearly killed himself in a motorcycle accident, he recognized that he needed to look more deeply at how he was leading his life. Sooner or later, a deeper part of us, our higher consciousness, drives us to reconnect with our feelings and our energy. Our addictions are our unconscious attempt to prevent that inevitable process from happening. By gently and compassionately investigating our addictions, we can soften the blow. By bringing awareness and understanding to them, we can undermine their power and appeal because inside us the desire for self knowledge is more powerful than our fears.

Gross and Subtle Addictions

In some cases, it is easy to identify what our addictions are. With chronic substance abuse, for instance, it is not so much of a problem to discover what we do to hide feelings as it is to find a way to stop it. But the addictions which most of us grapple with in our daily lives are the subtle ones – all the little ways that we dissipate our energy and prevent ourselves from contacting deeper feelings inside. Our self image, for example, is so deeply ingrained that we usually never stop to examine how we are using it to avoid feeling our pain. All the behaviors and attitudes that we hold onto for control are what make up our subtle addictions. The closer we look, the more these habitual behaviors and attitudes surface as addictive. Just about anything we do, even meditation, can become a way of avoiding rather than inviting our deeper fears and pain from arising.

Our addictions are tailored to our temperament. Some of us may pick the ingestive types – putting food, chemicals, sugar, etc. into our bodies in an attempt to ease our pain and anxiety that is created when the feelings or energy from the middle layer begins to penetrate and disturb our protection and control. One predominant form of addiction may be to structure our time so obsessively that we never have time to feel. Unless the feelings are very powerful, our incessant activity keeps us distracted and keeps the feelings buried. We can be deluded by our importance and by the importance of what we are doing – addicted to power and control. Power is like a drug that keeps us from our vulnerability. In a similar way, we can be addicted to our polished and socially rewarding image.

Looking more deeply into my own addictive behaviors, I discovered that speed has been a very significant addiction in my life – keeping busy, moving fast, crowding my time and my day with lists of things to do. Slowing down is frightening. Most of my life, I was too busy and too rushed to ever stop to consider it as an addiction. Western society is massively speed addicted. The Western mind is focused on achievement and progress – on getting somewhere. We may fortify our speed addiction with

137

substances such as coffee and sugar but the values of success and performance that keep the mind focused on "doing" rather than "being" are more insidious than the substances we ingest that keep us hurried.

With the subtle addictions, it is often not what we do but how we do it that identifies a behavior as addictive. Some year ago, I learned a way of making love that focuses on using love making as a way of staying connected and sharing deeply, taking the focus away from orgasm and onto sharing our moment to moment experience. This approach revealed to me how I was subtly using the energy of sexuality with my beloved as a kind of drug to prevent exploring and exposing my deeper fears of intimacy and inadequacy. Going under the addiction opened up vast new panoramas of closeness that I was afraid of.

Whatever addiction we use, the common denominator is that it prevents us from feeling vulnerable. We escape the moment because if we stayed present, we would be forced to confront our fears. Just slowing down to feel the moment, a slow process of changing my Western conditioning and integrating meditation into my life, gradually heals my addictions. In the past, I thought that with enough discipline, I could stop anything. But I found that discipline itself was one of my biggest addictions.

When I first came to India and met my spiritual master, I was following a highly disciplined spiritual path, fully convinced that if I only worked hard enough, I would attain. But instead of advising me to continue striving, he told me to do just the opposite – to drop all my striving and enjoy myself. My disciplines were simply a way I was fortifying my ego. "God," he said, "will find you". When I heard that, it struck me like a thunderbolt. I saw I was avoiding addiction with another addiction. Discipline alone is not a cure for addiction.

How to heal ourselves of our addictions? How to find a way to live our life in a gentle, but committed way, where we are no longer dissipating our energies, but remaining focused on growth? To answer that, I think, we need to take a deeper look at where these addictive behaviors come from.

The Fuel for Our Addictions

What is behind our addictions? Why do we choose to become unaware?

1) The Depth and Intensity of Our Unconscious Fears

Our fears are so deep and often so hidden that just the hint of allowing them to surface can be enough to cause us to want to keep the material buried. The more I understand about the inner child and in particular my own inner child, I can see that our wounds can be so terrifying, sometimes it seems a miracle that we ever find the courage to deal with any of them. Addictions shelter us from our anxiety and pain. We cannot push ourselves to allow this buried material to surface any faster than our being wants it to. We have to face ourselves with the utmost sensitivity and patience. Our addictions are one of the main ways that we keep some control over what comes up. No one but ourselves can know just how much to allow to surface.

When we finally decide to stop some form of addictive behavior, it is certainly going to bring up feelings that we have repressed. It is going to bring up the panic and the emptiness inside. Perhaps not right away, but sooner or later. At first, we may be filled with the enthusiasm of taking the step to stop a self-destructive behavior and we can enjoy a certain grace period. But the real difficulty usually starts after a few weeks. I have been with many friends who dropped smoking and their most difficult times came when, some weeks or even months down the road, they hit a set back – an experience that brought up their shame or insecurity - or they began to feel bored with "depriving" themselves, or started feeling too rigid and programmed. Any of these situations can cause us to revert. Without the addiction, we are much more raw. Our vulnerability comes to the surface.

Little things, which in the past we might have been able to ignore, suddenly bring up much panic. The panic is often cloaked in

139

irritation. We become much more sensitive to the unconsciousness around us, to violence and to insensitivity. Then it is easy to feel victimized and to want to give up or get angry at everyone. It is painful to expose our vulnerability. We have to really want it to come up. Given that our fears are so intense, I have found no simple way for dealing with addictions. There is no simple formula. Sometimes the most creative and loving thing we can do for ourselves is to simply stop. But at other times, the most loving approach is to do nothing but simply to watch our addictive behavior with as much awareness as possible.

Recently, I did a session with a woman who was suffering because her ex-boyfriend was no longer interested in her. He was somewhat ambivalent, but stated that all he wanted was a friendship. She could not accept that he no longer wanted her as a lover. She descended into a victim space and would beg for his attention, which he would give her sparingly. (I guess that many of us have been in this situation at some time.) She felt compelled to call him on the phone regularly and he always responded by rejecting her. She became more and more despondent and self-critical. Perpetuating this addictive behavior with him was doing her no good at all and there was no value in her watching it. She had to stop it. By continuing with the behavior, she was not letting herself feel the pain. Her suffering was part of the addiction; it was not a true pain experience. Instead, she needed to stop calling him and feel whatever that brought up.

But in contrast, often watching with awareness and continuing to do inner work is more than enough. A friend of mine is a heavy smoker. She knows it and she also knows that it is shielding her from her terror inside, but she can't stop. It would be violent for her to try and stop with discipline at this time in her life. She is doing intense work on herself and many frightening childhood traumas are surfacing. With this kind of commitment to her growth, most likely the addiction will drop by itself when she is ready.

Given the depth and intensity of our fears, the healing of any addiction may actually begin when we begin to accept that we are helpless to change anything unless we uncover the deep roots of our behaviors. We may not be able to actually change any of our obsessive behavior, but we begin to feel the pain. The woman in the example above may not be able to stop calling her ex-boyfriend, but when she comes out of automatic, she begins to feel the pain of that child inside who so hungers for love that she humiliates herself to get it. I can recall many times being caught in an obsessive behavior and there was simply nothing I could do but accept the helplessness.

2) Shame

A second and related source of our addictions comes from shame. It is as if there are two powerful forces inside us; one that carries our shame and says, "Why bother", and another that carries our seeker of truth that is saying, "Keep going for it." We suffer from a split. One part of us knows that there is value in persevering, in keeping the body healthy, in valuing our time, in following a growth program, in staying focused and working on ourselves. Another part of us wants to feel good now and does not want to sustain the commitment and focus.

Shame strengthens the part of us that does not have the commitment to grow because it has robbed us of self-value. Our shame, as we have seen, causes a deeply seated lack of trust in ourselves and in life. Until I could find some value for staying with the moment, even when it hurt, why bother? Until I found some value in persevering even during times of discouragement and failure, it was much easier to quit, space out or sabotage myself. *Only as I began to become more nourished by staying present, I discovered myself less drawn to things that gave me only immediate gratification.*

Perseverance, deferring gratification and the ability to tolerate frustration come from being loved and being taught to trust ourselves and our creative energies. If we are robbed of these, we lose a basic sense of trust and focus. Some of the most important messages that we can carry out of our childhood are that:

- Depth of feeling and allowing emotional pain is a valuable part of life because it brings depth and wisdom

- Nothing of value comes without effort and perseverance

- Life is precious – an opportunity to be creative and to give and receive love

I never learned the value of feeling pain; it was something that I had to pick up much later. But I did learn the value of perseverance. I remember my father spending hours practicing his flute and learning the languages of all the many different foreign countries he worked in while I was a child, and I remember my mother spending hours in her studio sculpting away at huge pieces of marble. I learned something of great value then. I also watched the vitality and enthusiasm with which my parents approached life and they infected me with that aliveness. I suspect that these lessons shielded me from ever being drawn to serious addiction even during moments of deep despair.

3) The Lack of Support for Growth and Meditation

One of the necessities of the spiritual seeker is to find an environment that provides support for growth. Even if we are highly disciplined, we can't do it alone. For that reason most spiritual masters have created a community around them to provide focus, structure and commitment. Without that support, we naturally lose the intensity and our subtle addictive behavior asserts itself. An environment that is focused on spiritual and emotional growth gives meaning to feel the pain and the emptiness that dropping addiction brings up.

The society and culture that most of us live in not only fails to help us with our inner work, it hinders it. Our soul and the soul of our culture is sick. We choose distraction and we sabotage our health and our energy with addictions because we have lost spiritual focus. Moreover, we have lost the trust in the spiritual process. If we want to move from addiction to awareness, we have to heal this soul wound. Just changing behavior doesn't bring us more awareness and unless there is a change in our awareness level, it doesn't last. If I stop doing something because I feel guilty about it, or by using discipline, it reoccurs eventually.

We are so addiction prone because, for the most part, Western culture has lost the understanding of the gentle relaxed discipline of spiritual growth. We have lost the understanding that is still preserved in the East in some spiritual traditions that life is an opportunity to go deeper into meditation, a spiritual path and process of learning spiritual lessons, some of which are extremely difficult and painful. Since this truth has not been part of most of our conditioning, we don't see the value of struggle and pain. I was touched by Sogyam Rinpoche's description, in his book, *The Tibetan Book of Living and Dying*, of a six-year-old boy about to enter the monastery waiting patiently for hours outside until the master called him in.

Our shame seeks us to look for the temporary high. We look for the momentary temporary experience of being out of our shame and fears without having to go through the painful process of healing it. It draws us to seek short cuts. We would like to be in our authenticity, aliveness and feelings without having to go through the shame and fear. To do that, we reach for any kind of compulsive and addictive behavior that makes us feel whole and alive again. Or we sink into a life of distraction without focus or intensity for growth.

We each have to find our own way to find support for our growth. Probably the best antidote of addiction is simply to find the support to become absorbed in our growth and in our search for truth. No matter how strong our compulsion to avoid, no matter how strong our inner resignation and laziness, our search for truth is stronger. Being absorbed in our inner work process is perhaps the most nourishing thing that we can do for ourselves. Our being starts to hum and then our addictive behavior naturally starts to fall away. It generates its own momentum. We gain self-respect.

Finding the Right Tension for the Bow

There is a Buddhist story about a famous archer who went to be with Buddha. He approached his spiritual work with great intensity, putting himself through the most rigorous austerities until he reached a point where he was nearly dead from fasting and hardships. Buddha watched this happening and finally called him to him. He asked him if he could remember from his days as an archer just how he tightened his bow. The archer told Buddha that when tightening his bow, he had to make it just right – neither too tight nor too loose. Buddha looked at him and said that he needed to approach the spiritual journey the same way – enough tightness to stay alert, but enough looseness to be relaxed. His bow, he told him, was much too tight.

Each of us has to learn to tighten our own bow. For some of us, it is too loose – we tend to become self-indulgent and sloppy and, for others, it is too tight, too disciplined and serious. In the past, I have kept my bow much too tight. I approached my journey with so much discipline and structure that humor and relaxation took periodic longer and longer holidays. Losing one's sense of humor is much too costly a price to pay for anything. I spent five years not eating any sugar, drinking any coffee, tea or alcohol. I thought that sexual energy needed to be transformed into "higher" energies and tried to learn all kinds of techniques to do that. I spent hours doing yoga and meditation and for years. I had the idea that doing anything else was a waste of time. This attitude also fed my repression and my righteousness and it kept me in control.

Then I would react to the control and rigor and go to the other extreme. I would go on seeker strike and indulge in all the things that I judged so intensely before (and after). No middle road, just a continuous process of bouncing back and forth. It was only after meeting my master that I recognized that growth is about letting go. What I was doing was creating tension. I was an intensity junky. It was time to face the fears and feelings that my addictions to discipline and intensity were covering up.

144

It seems that each situation has to be evaluated individually and we have to ask ourselves what is the most creative way to get in touch with the feelings underneath. At times, we do have to do something – move physically, get help from a therapist, change locations – whatever is appropriate. Other times, the most creative and growthful approach is to do nothing but just to watch. We all have our addictive behaviors. Some of them are more harmful to the body than others, some of them are easier to recognize than others. Those addictions that are socially acceptable or rewarded such as power, work and success, glittery material possessions, or an engaging façade, can often be the hardest to root out. But slowly I am finding that as I do the inner work and go deeper into meditation, it starts to become far more rewarding and gratifying to stay present and go into my feelings rather than to avoid them. In my experience, that is when the addictions start to fall away.

Exercise: Identifying and Working with Addictions

By using a meditative approach to work with addictions, the focus is not the behavior but uncovering the root of it, not on changing anything but watching and feeling what is underneath. This approach can start by looking closely for all the ways that you are choosing to avoid the moment and to avoid your deeper feelings. Investigating without pressure or judgment. These patterns are deeply ingrained and they cover wounds that your conscious mind strongly resists opening.

Here are some points to be aware of:

- Notice precisely what you do that takes you away from the moment

- What is the fear of staying present to the moment?

- What is being avoided right now?

- Does what you are doing feel like avoidance or is it creative?

- Notice what kinds of triggers (rejection, stress, disappointment, fear of failure) cause you to go into an addiction. (When our addiction has become habitual, the connection between the behavior and what you are avoiding can become obscured)

- Is there fear, anxiety or insecurity in this moment?
- How can you nourish yourself in a different way than the addiction?

******

Part 4

Working with Fear-
Ways We Can Change

Chapter 13

Bringing Back the Feelings

In this next section, we explore three tools to work with and heal our fears, to heal our panicked wounded child inside. The first is the ability to feel. Much of our fear arises from being disconnected from ourselves, from not being able to feel ourselves from moment to moment. Finding a way to bring back the feelings, to get under the shame and shock, under the numbness in our being and rediscover a richness of feeling states – anger, joy, grief, sexual aliveness, even genuine silence, is deeply empowering.

It is one thing to become aware of all the complex emotions that lie dormant in our middle layer – all the pain, repressed energy, shame, shock and fear that we hold inside, but it is quite another thing to be in direct contact with them. The question arises, how to access these feelings? That process is different for each of us. Each one of us has a different experience of shock and shame and how these wounds have affected our ability to feel. Because I have been such a shock person, it has always been an issue for me; how to feel without pushing, without pressure, without "doing" something?

The ways that we have developed in working with people and helping them to access their feelings have been strongly influenced by my own work with myself. This has led to six principle ingredients:

- Creating an atmosphere without judgment or pressure

- Healing through understanding and acceptance

- Creating space to feel and validate our shame and shock

- Creating an energy of commitment and focus

- Listening and trusting the body

- Reawakening our inner knowing

Taking the Pressure Off

If we have experienced significant shock and repression of our feelings, we may have great difficulties getting in contact with them. I've never had an easy time feeling or expressing my feelings. I have judged myself for not being able to cry easily, or for not being readily in touch with my anger. Sensitive people, I always thought, could cry and powerful people get angry. I felt that I was neither. I felt handicapped. The slightest bit of pressure to feel and I would shut down even further.

Now, I recognize that I was not alone in my fears. *Unless our child inside feels that he or she has not the slightest pressure to produce feelings or to change in anyway, we will not open to our deepest spaces inside.* We may even be able to express anger and sadness, but our core will remain in hiding. We will move into a compensation to please or make contact with the therapist. Instead, we need to be validated in our own tempo and given absolute space to discover our own way to feel and express emotions. A psychiatrist I saw while in my psychiatry residency was the first person who helped me to see that my difficulty with feeling and expressing emotions was only because feelings were seldom, if ever, expressed in my family. That was the first time a therapist had validated my relationship to feelings and, with that validation, I began the process of taking the pressure off myself.

He also explained to me that one cannot push the unconscious. Everything comes when it is ready. I believed that if I didn't push, nothing would happen. Furthermore, he said that he didn't need to see me crying to know that I was feeling pain. That was all I needed to hear to open to my pain because, perhaps for the first time, I felt deeply seen and understood. My feelings were locked inside me and my pushing was a compensation that only took me further away from them; it was more related to my conditioning than to my authenticity. I was still being "the good boy".

With gentleness, our inner child will come out. He or she needs to feel that there is no threat, no pressure and no expectation. Then in his or her own time and own way, the child inside will come out, very slowly perhaps, but reliably.

Bringing Understanding and Acceptance

When we can understand what we have been through; it paves the way for our energy to be released naturally and spontaneously. Until I learned about shock, I still judged my numbness and my paralysis in the face of fear. I was okay as long as I was "in my energy", but I was not okay when I was gripped in fear. Now I know that this idea of "being in my energy" was not really my energy at all; it was compensation. True, after a strong and energetic cathartic session, I had tapped into a collective vitality and aliveness. I felt empowered, I became aware of how I had compromised myself and suddenly I felt new courage to assert my boundaries. All this was very important, but it still did not go to my core.

I felt a bit like a yo-yo. Energized and assertive at times, collapsed and frozen at others. I was not consistently developing my sense of integrity and centeredness. But understanding shame and shock, validating my child inside who was frozen in fear when confronted with judgment, violence, or pressure, changed that. I began to understand and appreciate myself at a much deeper level. I started no longer evaluating myself according to how alive I seemed. I began to appreciate the deeply sensitive being inside who went into hiding and covered his fears with a mask of a highly competent "doer". Our healing comes from falling into a place of full understanding where there is tremendous acceptance and space, without the slightest pressure or criticism for how we should be. Out of that understanding, we can return to a true centeredness and inner silence.

Feeling the Shock and the Shame

Shock and shame are states of our emotional nature that we need to validate and feel. If we don't validate these states, we condemn ourselves for being collapsed and shamed, or we escape from the shame and shock into some form of compensation. There is no room to go further in either case. We have to start where we are, not where we think we should be. *If shame or shock comes, that is what we have to feel.* But to do that, we have to apply a different quality to how we normally feel ourselves.

Normally, we feel when some strong emotion pulls us inside. The power of that emotion is enough to tune us in, to take us away from our habitual and unconscious protection and into the moment. But when we are in shame or shock, we can't feel emotion – it is blocked. All we sense is an absence of feeling because that is how shock and shame work. Then, as I have mentioned before, we judge ourselves for not feeling, for not "being in our energy", for being paralyzed and numb, or for not being able to express ourselves. This doesn't help much for feeling anything. It is a vicious cycle. *We can get out of the cycle by validating and feeling the collapse.*

Still, we don't like ourselves when we are not able to say what we would like to say and be how we would like to be. Somebody says or does something and we feel hurt.

Later, we might think of a million things we would have liked to have said, but at the moment, we are in shock. Then we berate ourselves for not standing up for ourselves. There is nothing to do in that situation except feel the shock and the shame. That is precisely what we need to experience. Until we allow ourselves to feel the shame and shock wound and give ourselves the space to go into it totally, it will never heal. We can spend a lifetime in compensation, avoiding the uncomfortable feeling of the shame or shock, but it won't help us to grow. What helps is to go into the wound. We will continue to create experiences in our life that bring it up just so that we can go into it.

As I mentioned earlier in the chapters on shame and shock, these two have very specific states, unique to each of us, that we can feel in the body. But we have to take the time to learn what that feeling is like. I can offer an example from my own experience. I have a friend who almost always has put me in shock when I am around him. For one reason or another, I would feel shamed and inferior every time I was with him. After each time we spent together, I went away feeling terrible inside, never knowing why. But I began to recognize the symptoms. First there are the thoughts – my self judgments, self doubts and insecurities. And then the body sensations; I felt a hollowness in my solar plexus, a powerlessness and low energy. I felt heavy and foggy without dignity, feeling that I had compromised and given my power away.

Part of recognizing the feelings of shame and shock is also identifying what triggers them. Spending time with family, for example, is usually a great shame and shock trigger. I have also recognized that most of the time, my shame was provoked by opening to people who were out of touch with their own shame and their wounded inner child. Because of our wounds and past experiences, our child often neurotically seeks approval from those who are in authority and/or we look up to. We become a victim and then invite shame and abuse.

It is not easy to feel either shame or shock. They are uncomfortable feelings that we would rather not feel. They are also hard to feel because they are not energetic. In fact, they deprive us of our energy. It is much easier to feel something that is energetic such as sadness, anger, sexuality or joy. Shame and shock by their very nature are devoid of energy. Nonetheless, these two phenomena are feeling states that must be given full space and recognition. They are worth the same amount of inner growth dollars as any other "feeling". Unless we give ourselves the space and acceptance to feel them, we don't allow anything else to happen. We have to be exactly where we are, without judgment or expectation.

Creating Commitment and Focus

When we have a sincere intention to heal, our whole life becomes an arena for bringing back feelings that we have buried. When we begin to become aware of the wounds we carry, all the feelings and aliveness we have repressed naturally begin to surface. Even the most seemingly trivial events in our life will provoke feelings and reaction. A conversation with a parent, lover or friend now can become a powerful awakening to feeling. Once I began to work with my wounded child, I had much fewer casual conversations with anyone, particularly those close to me. Every time I spoke with my parents, I could feel what it provoked.

It is our commitment to heal that alone ushers in feeling. It is as though we are asking existence to come to our aid to help us rekindle our feeling nature and it does. In our workshops, we simply ask our participants to let go of any pushing or expectation about feeling, asking them to replace it only with a willingness to heal and to stay present with whatever comes up. We do much of the emotional work by placing people on a mattress alone and guiding them through meditations into hidden rage, grief, sexuality, joy and silence. We begin by asking them to bring their focus and intention to the moment and to the process they are about to be taken into.

We ask them to allow this moment to be the most important moment in their life and to be open to allowing existence to bring them whatever they need. With that commitment, focus and willingness to be present, they need to do nothing else. Then we gently direct them into a journey to explore inner wounds, using words and music and sometimes breathing to focus and intensify the exploration. This approach often unleashes tremendous feelings in a way that is safe and unique to each person.

Listening and Trusting the Body

I stopped believing that I couldn't feel when I became more aware of my body. I was registering my feelings right there all the time and all I needed to do was stop and pay attention. We carry this treasure trove inside all the time just waiting to be tapped into. We stopped trusting the body when we stopped trusting ourselves. Teaching how to relearn this simple tool, learning to tune into the subtle sensations in the body, is one of the cornerstones of this approach to bringing back the feelings.

What does this mean – listening and trusting the body? Our body is magnificently sensitive and is much more in touch with our deeper self than our mind.

Our body is not riddled with self criticism and judgments. *It just feels.* These subtle signals from the body give continual information about our emotional states. The greater our shame and shock, the more subtle these signals may be, but if we can learn to tune in closely, we can read them no matter how buried and muffled they may have become. It becomes an ongoing meditation for each of us to rediscover our own signals. A big part of this meditation is learning how to get our noisy, self-critical mind out of the way, so that we can listen again.

This process of learning to listen and trust the body again is highly subjective. Feelings such as sadness, anger, joy, or fear may have common reoccurring body sensations in specific lo-cations in the body that tend to be universal, but their presentation is unique for each of us. It's our body and our shame and shock and that is unique. We all have our own discovery to do to identify our fear, our anger, our sadness and our silence. It is an exciting project.

Awakening the Inner Knowing

Underneath all of these different feelings – sadness, fear, anger, joy – there is something even deeper, an inner knowing that we also lost. This inner knowing is like a guiding light that tells us every minute what nourishes, what fits, what feels right and what doesn't. It helps us know where we want to be, what we want to do and where we want to go. We lost touch with this feeling because generally it was not supported in childhood. We seem to recreate experiences today as a way to test and challenge us to bring it back and learn to trust it again.

For as long as I can remember, I have mistrusted my intuition. I have always known inside which people nourished me and made me feel relaxed and which people made me tense and anxious. Yet I could not trust it. I have doubted myself so much that, over and over again, I would compromise, humiliate or invalidate myself, simply because I was not trusting my inner feelings. Often, I was in situations where I should have stood up for myself and said, "No!" but I didn't trust myself.

Our instincts are so clear and so simple when we can pay attention and trust the signals. The signals often come from just listening and feeling the body. It knows and is telling us in its own way when we are feeling loved, whom we feel comfortable spending time with and opening with, and what nourishes us. Our mind can be saying all kinds of things, listening to everything that others may be saying, but the body knows what we need and what feels right.

Learning to listen to our inner knowing also involves learning to listen and balance two parts of us; *that part of us that wants freedom and another that wants and needs security and safety.* Our freedom side can be pressuring us to make quite dramatic changes in our lives, calling us into unknown territory away from the beaten path. Our freedom side wants to set us free from repression and self compromise, whatever the cost. It wants to pull us out of a relationship that may have become unhealthy, or to make changes in our work situation or living conditions if they no longer support our growth.

But these changes may overload the side of us that needs security – our vulnerable, panicked child. We have to also honor our inner child's need for security, safety and gentleness, the part of us that is afraid to break the bonds and afraid of the unknown. If we learn to be sensitive to both sides, the growth happens without violence. We learn to move at a pace that is in harmony with both sides of us. We will make the moves and the changes we need to make, but the movement can become more of a flow.

Combining Intensity and Sensitivity

We each have our own journey of "bringing back the feelings". But it is my experience that regardless of our differences, the qualities of deep acceptance and understanding, gentle patience and steady presence allow our sensitivity to emerge together with all the vitality that has always been inside. We have searched for a method of inner growth and life change as refined as the instrument that we are playing on. The sensitivity that we hold inside is exquisite. At the same time, the passion and intensity of our feelings are powerful. In the therapy work I have done in the past, I have often compromised my sensitivity for intensity. But as my meditation grows, that kind of compromise is no longer possible. Integrating intensity and sensitivity has motivated how I work with myself and the work we offer to others.

In the past, I needed to put myself in strong cathartic experiences to connect with my anger. They served their purpose. At times, it may be essential for any of us to create powerful experiences that take us deeper into our grief and buried pain. But learning to "bring back the feelings" is basically an ongoing moment to moment process of watching and feeling the little things that trigger anger, pain, joy or pleasure. This is a meditation that goes on every waking hour; feeling the subtle body sensations that each one arises, observing what triggers them and how, watching how they affect the mind, noticing what they do to our energy, noticing our attachment to joy and pleasure and our rejection of anger or pain and watching each one of them change.

Meditation: Bringing Back the Feelings

Allow yourself to find a comfortable position for your body – sitting or lying down. Allow your arms and legs to relax and slowly begin to go deeply inside. Relax and go inside. Gently allow yourself to tune into your body. Allow your focus to become directed on your body.

157

Begin by bringing your attention to the heart. Feel this as a seat of much compassion and acceptance. Perhaps you can feel this quality of acceptance as an energy radiating from your whole being. Imagine bathing your whole being in this energy of acceptance, in this compassion, allowing this acceptance to give greater inner space, more and more inner space, replacing any judgments with spaciousness, so that now there is more room to watch yourself and to feel yourself. There is space to watch and to accept, space to feel; watching and feeling whatever is there, whatever you find.

With this spaciousness, this acceptance, you can begin to notice what is going on this moment. You can notice what is going on in the body. Stepping back a little and bringing all your awareness to the body. Noticing the body; what pulls your attention? Is there anywhere that you feel some tension, some tightness? If so, observe it, feel it. See if you can let go of any judgments, allowing yourself just to be with it and to feel it. Noticing with openness, curiosity, gently letting go of any judgment or expectation.

Notice any thoughts that you are having at this moment. How do these cause your body to feel? What sensations arise with these thoughts? How do they make you feel? All part of watching and feeling, watching and allowing. Becoming very sensitive to the body, to the messages from the body. It is feeling, sensing all the time, each moment – very sensitively, very subtlety, very accurately. Such a close connection of our thoughts with our feelings, with our body, with the sensations, moment to moment, each moment in the body.

Being very present – right here, right now. With the body, with the thoughts, with the sensations. Watching, feeling, and allowing whatever is there. Feeling it. We can tune in at any time. Allowing this meditation to be ongoing – always an awareness of the body. Becoming more trusting of the body, just learning to listen, gently and closely. Such a sensitive instrument, helping us to tune in each moment. Listening to our truth each moment. Every emotion with its own body sensation each moment.

158

Beginning a process of tuning into your inner world. A world of feelings, sensations. Noticing the thoughts any thoughts that come, again with total acceptance. Thoughts of judgment, thoughts about anything, just observing and then returning to noticing the feelings inside.

Beginning to become familiar with sensations and feelings in the body, bringing them into your belly, with lots of space and allowing. Very sensitive to even the slightest sensation or feeling. Nothing needing to happen, just feeling and allowing. Becoming familiar with allowing and giving space, without judgment, without needing to change anything. Just feeling, tuning in, discovering your inner world.

And now, allowing yourself to come back. Coming back gently and slowly but keeping this awareness of the body with you all the time. Coming back and opening your eyes.

******

Chapter 14

Passion for Living -
Igniting the Life Force with Energy and Risk

Katarina, a participant in one of our workshops, was sharing that she was having difficulty not going to sleep whenever we did a guided meditation on working with shame or shock. She had done several of our workshops and was feeling discouraged. Amana and I shared with her that the problem was that she was missing energy. She had become used to feeling and seeing herself as a person with low energy and did not realize that this might interfere with her healing. Amana encouraged her to begin including in her regular life, on a daily basis, activities which would stretch her to bring more aliveness into her body – whatever she liked, for example swimming, yoga, jogging, working out, dancing or walking in nature.

Waking Up the Passion

We consider this to be a vital factor in transformation and inner growth. *It takes energy to become aware and it takes energy to overcome the downward pull of our shame and our fears.* Shame and fear often depresses our life energy and allows more space for the negative thoughts of shame and fear to take over our mind. We need to use some effort to get out of this destructive pattern. The ways that we choose to engage and raise our energy can involve activities that directly call on the body to exert energy. Life energy in the body feels so good that the more energy we put into the body, the more it gets used to holding and the more it longs for it on a regular basis. When we get used to using and exerting our body, it becomes an incredible resource to overcome the deep programming of our shame and fear.

The energy that we generate by moving the body can also spread to other areas of our life and helps us to feel a passion for life and for living that we might have lost touch with because of our wounding. Physically moving the body can often be the first step

161

to igniting this passion, which then extends to making our daily life full of creativity and fun – passion to grow, to learn and discover new things, to travel and to try out new creative ventures such as learning to sing, sing, paint or make music. This can also happen the other way around. We become more passionate about living because of our creativity and it spreads to becoming more aware and attentive to the life energy in the body. It may also be important to seek out support and guidance when we are taking this new leap journey in passionate living. Many clients and friends have told us that they have started with a fitness trainer, or a singing, music or dance teacher and this has inspired them to overcome their reluctance and fears.

Taking Risks to Awaken the Passion

I remember once watching a movie with Bill Murray and Richard Dreyfus called *"What About Bob"*. Richard Dreyfus plays a psychiatrist who has just written a book called "Baby Steps", which he gives to his patient, Bill Murray, to help him overcome his fears. He never reads the book, (or if he did, it was off screen), but just carrying it around is enough to give him courage. The concept of "baby steps" fits so perfectly for using risk to heal our shame and shock. That is all that we have to take – baby steps. The size of the step we take or the result doesn't make any difference. The smallest step into engaging our fear produces energy. Energy produces growth and transformation. And that is what we are interested in.

The energy to cast off our cloak of shame comes from our life force. Understanding and acceptance is the passive pole, risking and waking up the life energy is the active pole of our healing process. It provides the energy we need to heal by igniting our life energy. This energy comes from the "hara", from our center. If we allow it to flow out of us, it naturally asserts our dignity and our creativity. Our shame holds down this life force, imprisoning the vital energies that were shut down in childhood. As we have seen, we struck an unconscious bargain to limit this energy in return for love and approval. Now, whenever we want to claim it back, move out of our zone of comfort and familiarity into the unknown, we have to face tremendous guilt and fear. We can continue to live within the limits defined by our shame, fear and guilt. Or we can test them by taking risks.

Risking Brings Fear and Shame

Amana and I were staying at a Spa Hotel in the Alps eating our hearts out after a long day of hiking. At the table next to us was a young German couple who had also spent the day hiking, but unknowingly took on a longer and tougher hike than they had planned. The boyfriend was afraid of heights and, on the way back, there was an 800 meter drop that they had to climb down with the assistance of ropes tied to the rocks. His body was shaking with fear and his girlfriend, who had more experience, had to hold him so he could make it. *There is an easy way to tell if we are risking. It brings up fear.* Each new step away from the known and familiar brings up this fear. I have invited and sought out challenges because I did not want to be ruled by my fear. At the same time, I have had to learn to respect, accept and validate the fear. In risking, we have to strike a balance between venturing into the new and accepting the part of us that is afraid.

Risking also brings up our shame, doubts and insecurities, because our child inside remembers that in the past challenging the status quo brought up some form of punishment, humiliation, judgment or deprivation of love. Our child also believes that if it keeps our life energy small, there is less danger of being re-traumatized. That is no small obstacle to overcome. Risking will trigger some deep primal fear and in the mind of our child, this can be terrifying. But the price of staying in the child's fears is too high. Each time that I have found the courage to take the risk and go with my life energy, passion and aliveness, my negative beliefs begin to shatter and the repercussions are never what I thought they would be. It has always moved me in the direction that my being naturally wanted to take. Of course, that is after the fact. Each new hurdle brings up the same dilemma, but we have to find a way to take the jump. Taking even the smallest risk begins to heal this wound. There is no wound too big that it cannot be healed by risking. It restores our confidence, our courage and our dignity.

Three Areas of Risk

There is no formula for what a risk will be. For each of us, the areas of risk at any moment in our life are different; one person's risk can be another person's addiction. But there are three areas where risking will change the quality of our life:

- *A willingness to be more vulnerable* – to open, to explore our defensive and protective mechanisms and to expose our dark sides and our secrets

- *A willingness to live with a higher level of honesty* – to honor our commitments and promises and to share even when we are afraid

- *A willingness to be more alive* – to assert our creativity and go through the fears, the shame, the discouragements and the disappointments that inevitably come up whenever we risk to be alive and creative

In all these areas, it is not the results that are important but our willingness to test our limits because that sends a message to our higher consciousness that we are ready to enter a new level of awareness. In all of these three areas, there is bound to be fear. Let's take a look at some of these areas of risk.

1) Risking to Be Vulnerable

I pick this one to start because generally risk is associated with something more male oriented. But now I recognize that, at least for me, the greatest risk is to be vulnerable – to drop my controls, protections and to feel. I've done many things to test my fears and my limits, but nothing has been more frightening than taking the space to feel my fear and helplessness. It is still my most difficult area. I can find all sorts of ways to avoid dropping into my belly and feeling my helplessness, my dependency, my longing and my fears of rejection and abandonment. I can blame, fight, distract myself, eat sweets, watch movies and find ways to stay busy. But

164

when I am conscious enough to see myself in one of these behaviors, it becomes easier to feel the fear underneath.

One ingredient of risking vulnerability is to expose ourselves. We all hold secrets that lock us inside in isolation and self-condemnation. As Alice Miller has pointed out, in her book, *The Drama of the Gifted Child*, there is a wall of silence around our shame. To break down this wall of silence, we have to share; we have to speak the unspeakable. It may be terrifying, but once we do it, it seems to lift a huge weight from our soul. Furthermore, our shame has shut down our throat center. The shame has created an energy block in our throat and it prevents us from expressing ourselves. Taking the risk to open and expose ourselves helps to heal that wound.

At different times in my life I've been able to pit myself against nature in feats of daring, but to open and expose areas of my shame has always seemed to me much more difficult. First of all, until not so long ago, it just did not fit with my self-image to share my weaknesses or to expose my vulnerability. Often, because I have been used to isolating myself in my pain, I just don't know how to start to share. I don't find the words. But deeply buried in my wounded psyche and, I suspect, in the psyche of every anti-dependent, is the belief that no one will be there if I open. My vulnerability was so deeply hidden that he did not even know what it was like when someone was there.

Slowly, I have had to learn the tools of opening. It has been a slow, but rewarding process. I have found that with some people, the words and the feelings just come. Something in their receptivity, presence and their own experience seems to invite and trigger my openness. In other situations, I not only find it hard to share, I am not even in touch with the feelings. Realizing this has helped me not to judge myself so much when I can't express and to wait to be with those where my heart can open more easily.

We have to be mindful of our expectations. There are never any guarantees that when we do finally open, someone will be there to listen and will totally understand us. If we have this expectation, then it's not a true opening and rejection often follows. But when the pain of isolation becomes even greater than the fear of humiliation or rejection, we come out of our cave. We make the choice to open anyway. When we can start to open without the charge of expectation, we are on the road to finding the understanding that we so yearn for.

2) Risking to Be Honest

When I risk to be honest, I also risk being alone. It is certainly safer to stay hypnotized in denial and live in false harmony. Then I don't have to run the risk of having someone cut me off or get angry with me. I also don't have to risk making changes in my life that would rock the boat and cause me to lose something or someone. But I don't like myself when I am dishonest. In the past, I had adjusted myself to living at a level of dishonesty because I didn't know any better. Dishonesty was what I had always been surrounded with. Every social situation I was ever exposed to as a child was full of dishonesty – people talking behind other people's backs and covering the duplicity with a mask of politeness. Our conditioning was not to risk unpleasantness and disharmony. It was better to pretend than to create friction. *As a result of this kind of dishonesty, our life energy suffers.*

Learning how to be honest requires a radical re-conditioning of how to be with people. It has been - and still is - often terrifying for me to say something to someone that I fear will meet with resistance, anger or rejection. I don't like confrontation or anger. But the alternative is worse. The price of not saying what I need to say has become too great. I build resentment and close off. I feel the friction and I get cautious and collapsed in my energy. For all of us coming out of shame and shock, one of the most difficult things to do is to live and express our truth and confront someone if we have been hurt.

When there is dishonesty between friends and lovers, it destroys the relationship. As the dishonesty grows, so does the distance

166

and the resentment. With lovers, the sexual connection suffers first because it is hard to lie in love making. Eventually, unless we clean things up, we don't have a relationship anymore; we have a dry, painful arrangement. It becomes a question of priorities. With dishonesty, we can, at least for a time, stay safe. Honesty threatens that. I also include as honesty, being accountable – to do what we say we are going to do. And finally, to learn to finish what we start. Both of these qualities take courage but build a tremendous amount of self-esteem.

It is always a dance between our frightened child who needs safety and security and our freedom seeker who wants truth. We have to learn to integrate and be sensitive to both. Our shame has taught us to tolerate a lower level of honesty because we are accustomed to having low integrity and self-esteem. Our wounded self does not believe it will survive by living honestly. But once we decide that we don't need to continue living with this negative, shame-based self-image, things change.

3) Risking to Be Alive

One night, several years ago, I was listening to my master speak about authenticity and aliveness. He was saying that in all of eternity there will never be another person just like us. All we have to do is discover our individuality and gently and lovingly live it. How many of us, I thought to myself, ever realize and live out this truth in our lives? We all have a choice every moment whether to be present and alive. But our shame has caused us to trivialize ourselves and our life. *Often we minimize the preciousness of every moment that we have to be alive; we don't recognize or value the beautiful and unique contribution that our creativity has to make and we don't honor the significance of each of our intimate connections.*

Our energy has been repressed. Not only were we shut down in the expression of our own authenticity - the flow of our sexual, assertive, blissful, and creative juices - but we also inherited all the fears and repression of our parents and the culture we were raised in. To overcome these repressive forces, we have to take

167

jumps into our energy. It is a struggle, but one that seems to get increasingly easier if we do it. It was an intense struggle for me to find the courage and confidence to become a seminar leader. I always knew somewhere that this is what I wanted and was gifted to do, but I didn't trust it. I still face the shame voices with each new seminar and with each new experience. But more and more, the creative forces take over and carry me along.

We have to go through fire tests of overcoming our shame wounds to be able to put out our creativity. The negative beliefs – that we are a basic failure, that we have nothing worthwhile to offer, that others are much better and that we will never make it – can be so strong that they can easily cripple us. There is a powerful creative energy inside each one of us that craves expression and we won't be content inside until we express it. We may have to do some healing before we connect with what it is and some more healing to find the courage to express it.

The same is true for any aspect of life energy. If we begin to explore our sexuality beyond what was permitted by our conditioning, our inner judge may begin to throw us lightening bolts of guilt and fear. If we get angry, the specter of a punishing father, mother, teacher, or priest may loom into our mind. If we begin to move into our power, there often comes a deep unconscious message that going any further will have serious and damaging consequences. If we expand with joy, if we indulge ourselves, if we do anything irresponsible, we may have to deal with the wrath of the whole collective culture that we were raised under. In short, to go from our comfortable false self into the real, vital and alive being that has always been there is very frightening. Little risks in this direction begin to shatter the power of all of these old programs. I don't think that my shame will ever disappear, but I can get some distance from it and then it no longer lives my life.

The Risk of Risking

When we start to work on ourselves, our repressed energy naturally starts to rise. It demands expression and it demands to be lived. If we take risks, it means trouble because it rocks the familiar and conventional life to which we may have become accustomed. In more extreme cases, deep inner work begins to demand more extreme life changes. Either we move with it, or we keep repressing it.

When we do risk and go with what wants to happen, we bring a burst of new vitality to our lives; the new is much richer than the old we gave up. That doesn't make it any less scary. Taking the risk to move with our energy involves tremendous courage. It means doing what we need to do, saying what we need to say and honoring the aliveness in our body. It means honoring and expressing the energy of each of our centers – sexual, emotional, assertive, creative, blissful and spiritual.

******

Chapter 15

The Meditative State of Consciousness

Recently, I was doing a session with someone who was telling me that he was driving away his lover because he was so desperately needy and demanding. Furthermore, he was jealous of her daughter because she was getting more attention from his lover than he was. He hated his neediness. It made him feel impotent and helpless and how could she possibly love and respect a man who could not be a man?

Under our compensations, there is a desperately needy child in most of us. That, at least, is my experience. *How do we live with that child, how do we share him or her and how can we heal him?* From the space of unconsciousness, we take our panic, our entitlement, our desperation and drop them into another's lap and say, "Here, take care of me". That's what children do and our child inside is just as desperate as he or she ever was. When we open to someone, these feelings begin to surface. To heal the wounded child, we have to learn to parent him. That parenting happens through cultivating the meditative state of consciousness.

This healing is not a doing – it is a watching and a feeling. It involves bringing to vulnerability and to all the dramas, pain and difficulties in our relating, the qualities of meditation. I have spent quite some time now describing the qualities of our state of consciousness when we are only identified with our panicked inner child – our fears, our entitlement strategies, our expectations, our shame and shock and our deep fears of abandonment. Fortunately, that is not the only state of consciousness inside us. There is also a buddha inside – a meditator. We can cultivate this latent buddha by cultivating our meditation.

Meditation gives us presence, an appreciation of who we are behind all our conditioned false personalities. When that meditative presence is there, something deep inside our panicked

171

child relaxes. As long as we are still living and identified with our false personalities - caretaker, pleaser, playboy, leader etc. - the fear-based child has no one to care for him or her. There is simply no real presence for the child that can ease his or her fears. But with the presence that grows through meditation, we are able to step back from the drama of our life and take it in with compassion. It gives us space, replacing the pressure and judgment that we have perpetually inflicted on ourselves with spaciousness.

Years ago, when I first went to India, I was already practicing Vipassana meditation. I thought that meditation meant sitting on a cushion, closing my eyes and watching my breathing. Sitting silently and going inside is probably the best way to nurture and cultivate our inner silence, but my master introduced me to a much vaster understanding for what meditation actually meant. It has taken many years to begin to understand that meditation is a state of being, a way of living and not something confined to a few hours on a zafu. It is probably one of my biggest lessons in life to learn that I don't have to do something to change or to be loved. Could it be that it is enough just to watch, feel and allow? That is the lesson I am learning about meditation.

The Qualities of Meditation that Allow Us to Heal

There are specific qualities that meditation brings to our con-sciousness that directly heal our woundedness. These qualities are: 1) witnessing, 2) understanding, 3) presence, 4) acceptance, 5) centering and 6) patience and trust. Let's take a look at each one.

1) Witnessing

Normally, when we are uncomfortable, in pain or in anxiety, our immediate reaction is to try to change the situation. In the "child state of consciousness", we do not tolerate these feelings well and want to "get out" of whatever is causing the pain. It takes quite some shift inside not to run away but instead to watch, feel and allow what is happening. When my pain or anxiety strikes, I can feel the strong pull of my child, but gradually I can also feel another space inside that is saying, "Wait, stop, feel; let it be just as it is. You can learn from staying with this experience and you have the space inside to hold it, feel it and be with it". This is a radical shift for our minds that have been so conditioned in the speedy, problem solving, doing energy of the Western world.

It is easy to become totally identified with our emotional process. Meditative consciousness is detached and that gives us the ability to *contain the panic, discomfort and grief that is inside*. With this detachment, we don't cut off from feeling, but give it more room to be. With more inner space, the desire to escape from the uncomfortable feelings is no longer so compelling. When I can trust that I have enough inner space to contain and *just stay present with the painful feelings*, I can choose not to run away. The meditator inside slowly gives me that trust.

For example, in the past, I defended myself from feeling pain when I separated for some time from my lover. I just didn't feel the pain of separation because I never allowed myself to get close enough. In fact, usually I was just relieved to have space and not be pressured to relate or open. Recently, that has changed. Now, separation brings pain, anxiety, even abandonment nightmares that have probably always been deeply buried inside. From doing this work, I recognize that no matter what I do, I can't avoid feeling emptiness and abandonment, so I am more inviting of the experience when it comes. I recognize the anxiety and know what is causing it. I don't judge it as much and I also know that there is enough inner space to allow it to come.

When we are witnessing, we are watching from a space where we can separate ourselves from the emotional drama but still feel. We are not going to die. Even more amazing, we discover that we are mystically cradled by existence. I would like to share with you a short description of witnessing, which I heard from my master once in a lecture:

"One has to start watching the body – walking, sitting, going to bed, eating. One should start from the most solid, because it is

173

easier and then one should move to subtler experiences. One should start watching thoughts and when one becomes an expert in watching thoughts, then one should start watching feelings. After you feel you can watch your feelings, then you should start watching your moods, which are even more subtle than your feelings and more vague.

The miracle of watching is that as you are watching the body, your watcher is becoming stronger; as you are watching the thoughts, your watcher is becoming stronger. When you are watching your moods, the watcher is so strong that it can remain itself, watching itself, just as a candle in the dark night not only lights everything around it; it also lights itself. To find the watcher is the greatest achievement in spirituality, because the watcher in you is your very soul; the watcher in you is your immortality."

Osho · The Golden Future

2) Understanding

The word, "understanding" has an energy to it. Just saying the word communicates the energy. It covers our experience with a blanket of compassion. When there is understanding, there is acceptance and with acceptance comes restfulness. Understanding is another quality that naturally springs from meditation. It comes because in meditation, the focus is not to do anything but just to *see things as they are* – just stepping back far enough to get a good look.

Meditation gradually helps me to soften how I look at things and, in that softening, I have been able to understand my inner child. As long as I was evaluating myself according to how well I did at things, how much I had accomplished, there wasn't room for understanding my inner child. Meditation brings out the feminine inside of us where our compassion and understanding can flower. My harsh judging mind arose out of the strict standards that I was applying to myself – standards based on success and failure. Meditation has slowed me down and is gradually giving more space for the gentleness inside.

It is this side of me that has space to understand my shame and shock. It cuts through the harsh judgments. Slowly, with this kind of consciousness, we can take the heat off ourselves and stop feeling guilty and inadequate about our failures. With meditation, success and failure become less relevant. We begin to see life as a growth process and all our struggles are part of that process. Before developing understanding, I viewed all my actions as a test of my self-esteem. It created tremendous pressure because I was trying to become who I was supposed to become instead of who I really was. In a sense, my life was an intense struggle to prove myself. It was like being in a constant war with my inner and outer judges.

3) Acceptance

As we go inside and explore, we start to see things about ourselves that are often not so easy to accept. It is no wonder, given the depth of our unconsciousness, that we avoid looking at ourselves. "Our stuff" – our compulsions and obsessions, the ways we are insensitive to others, the ways we hurt ourselves, and the ways we repeat the same behavior and patterns repeatedly – is painful to recognize. We slip continually back to our childhood state, to our strategies, to our feelings of hopelessness, to our entitlement, to our protections and to our shame and shock. When that happens, the judging mind is always there to condemn us. When we recognize something inside that we don't like, the natural impulse is to want to change it.

In the meditative approach to healing, change is secondary. What matters is that *we watch and accept what is* – as scientists of the soul, of the inner world. Watching and accepting are the instruments of the search. If we are focused on change, we are not living in the moment and we cannot discover ourselves. We will continue to succeed and then fail, to shame ourselves, to compromise our dignity, to be insensitive, unconscious and irresponsible over and over again. It is not easy to watch all this. We would much rather that it stops. In my experience, real change happens slowly. It happens by itself once we have found the ability to watch and to accept.

4) Presence

Presence is the essence of meditation – *learning to stay with the moment, watching and feeling it just as it is.* Our fears, panic and lack of trust make it extremely hard to do that. When I started meditating, I focused diligently on watching my breath, my thoughts and the sensations in my body, just as my teachers were instructing me to do. (Good, diligent student that I have always been.) I evaluated myself on how well I could do that. If I was restless and unfocused, I judged myself. I never realized that my restlessness was a symptom of the fears of my inner child that were being provoked for one reason or another.

Uncovering the panic in my child has made the practice of meditation a very different story for me. Now, I recognize where much of my distractedness, anxiety and lack of peace of mind come from, not just when I am sitting in meditation, but all the time. These moments test my ability to be present with what is – with all the panic of my wounded child. Inner child work brought a very new understanding of presence and meditation for me; more difficult, but much more alive and rich.

In my experience, making a gentle commitment to stay present is deeply healing for our inner child. Our fears disconnect us from ourselves. Learning to stay present heals that wound. That is easy when we are feeling comfortable and content inside, but it's extremely difficult when pain or fear is triggered. Normally, when something is affecting us emotionally, we feel it in the belly. For most of us, this mechanism was invalidated and destroyed as a child. But when we lose this mechanism, it prevents us from staying with our feelings each moment.

Validating and honoring ourselves begins with recognizing, allowing and accepting whatever is happening in our body, in our belly, each moment. That is how we begin to come home. The first step, even before we can express anything, is to connect inside. For someone like me coming out of shock and shame, the perception that I am angry or sad was a total mystery. Asked to express or share feelings, I went deeper into shock. When I focused on learning presence, I started to release the pressure of having to express anything until I could connect with myself inside.

Presence is non-judgmental awareness. The moment I validate what is happening instead of judging myself for not feeling something else, or for not feeling more, I create space for more to be revealed.

Since I didn't have this space as a child and didn't give it to myself as an adult, I had to start afresh. Now, instead of, "Feel this and do that!" it becomes, "Let's just see what is happening in there." I can feel the cloak of shame and begin to trace it to an event, or a conversation, to a put down from someone or a disappointment. I can begin to feel the hurt or the anger of being shamed and to respond. I could also notice more often when I "leaked my energy" - when I was compromising my dignity for respect, for approval, or for love. I noticed what provoked the leak and just by cultivating this awareness the leaks plug up. The starting point was to recognize the importance of staying present.

5) Centering

Probably our biggest challenge in healing our child is simply learning to give ourselves the space to feel without reacting. We call this "holding the feelings". Instead of reacting, if we can just stay with what we are feeling, allowing it to deepen and to keep watching, something quite amazing happens. Something inside begins to relax. When the uncomfortable feelings come, every cell in our body wants to turn off the feeling, our mind begins to concoct all kinds of terrifying thoughts and we find ways to escape. By ignoring these thoughts and ignoring our impulse to run away, or fight, we cultivate our meditative state of consciousness. This process is transformative.

But it takes a certain ability to stay centered. Shame robbed us of our contact with our center. Tuning into the sensations of our body and to our belly gradually, but progressively, takes us back to our center. Being connected with our center is the source of our self-esteem and our groundedness. It enables us to hold the panic and not react with it. In my own process, perhaps because my shock is so deep, this comes very slowly. Sometimes I feel overwhelmed by the panic and it takes every ounce of awareness to watch. But I can also sense that the time spent in slowing down, sitting silently and tuning in is healing this. It just takes being patient with myself.

6) Patience and Trust

In the world of meditation, there is a different sense of time than say on the Los Angeles Freeway. It wouldn't do much good to try to convince someone holding his cellular phone and stuck in traffic on the 405 of the truth in the ancient Zen saying, "Sitting silently, doing nothing, Spring comes and the grass grows by itself." Patience has never been one of my fortes either. My mother used to tell all my teachers as a child, "One thing I can tell you about him is that he can't sit still. He always has to be doing something."

But in healing our inner child, nothing happens quickly. It is a slow, delicate process. The same is true in meditation. If we meditate with a goal, we soon grow tired and frustrated. In both cases, doing inner child work and going deeper into meditation, we just have to enjoy the process. We can spend long periods of time without noticing any overt changes in our behavior, in our attitudes toward ourselves and toward others. It can get frustrating and discouraging. But then all of a sudden, something dramatic changes; our work begins to flow, the outer rewards come in, or we create a deeper and more nourishing love life.

In the earlier days of my therapy work with myself, the changes seemed more dramatic. I was doing strong processes that dramatically opened repressed energy and moved much energy. But once I started co-dependency and inner child work, dealing with my shame and shock, my fears of abandonment and intimacy, exploring spaces of deep fear and emptiness, the changes have never seemed so quick or dramatic. Yet I feel they are deeper. The earlier work satisfied my hunger for fast results, but with the inner child work, I have had to learn patience.

I can see that my rushing, planning and ambitious mind come from my panicked child. Patience comes out of a deep trust that everything that is meant to happen and needs to happen, will happen and will happen in its own time. Patience and trust are intricately entwined. Sitting in meditation with my master and feeling the qualities of timelessness, slowness and centeredness that he emanates is slowly teaching me patience and trust. No rush, no agenda, nothing but this moment. Carried to the arena of relating and healing our co-dependency, this quality has profound impact.

On some level, our inner child is going to remain hungry and panicked. What changes is that our meditative state becomes stronger and our trust goes deeper. It is not even a matter of trusting someone in particular, but we develop a space of trusting in general. I have this space in moments. With more meditation, it seems to grow. No one can give this to me; I have to find it inside. It is a treasure hunt; this calmness at the core of our being that eclipses all our emotional traumas, fears and doubts.

Growing from Panic to Meditation

Meditation is one of the strongest resources available for healing and finding ourselves. It gives us inner space to stay with the fear and the pain inside. Life can hand us some devastating blows. But, instead of responding to adversity, disappointment, rejection and loss with the attitude that we are a helpless recipient of life's and other people's malice, we can accept it. We can let go of being a victim. Pain can make us bitter. But if we regard it as a blessing that takes us deeper inside, we can make sense of it.

If we begin to take time to go inside and feel what is there, we cultivate the ability to listen. We become more sensitive to our own needs and feelings and to those of others. Before developing meditative consciousness, all we really have is a panicked child covered up with an unconscious avoiding compensating "adult". Meditation turns this "adult" into a real adult. Our meditativeness enables us to embrace our child with an energy that allows him or her to feel seen, cared for and secure.

Meditation does not need to be rigorous, serious or strenuous. It is just a celebration of our nature. Gradually, the more we cultivate this inner space, the more it opens and becomes something that we need and yearn for. Gradually, meditation just seems to become something that is part of our life, not just as a practice that we do for so many minutes a day, but a whole way of life. Awareness of our body, of our thoughts, feelings and actions becomes a focus of our life.

Meditation: Cultivating the Witness

I suggest that you have a friend read this to you or read it slowly into a tape recorder and listen afterwards.

Begin by finding a comfortable position for your body. Close your eyes and take a deep breath, inhaling deeply and exhaling. Begin to allow yourself to relax, going inside, beginning to slow down and relax. If sleepiness arises, just give yourself a gentle message to stay alert and attentive, alert and aware as you relax and go inside.

Now, allow your attention to focus on your breath and begin to watch the breathing. Noticing how it enters and leaves the body completely beyond your control. Entering and leaving totally on its own. And watching the breath, begin to feel yourself falling into its natural rhythm, coming in and going out on its own. Each moment a new breath, coming in and going out, rising and falling.

Seeing how the breath comes and goes completely on its own, you can begin to let go, letting go of the need to control, letting go of the idea that you have to be constantly directing, or controlling, or protecting. Letting go. A breath enters and leaves the body entirely on its own. It entered the body at the moment of your birth and it will exit the body on the moment of your death. It comes and it goes on its own, governed by a power much more awesome than your will.

The breath can bring us to a place where we can watch, just as a witness. So continue sinking into this inner space deep inside, a place where you can watch, just watch. And from this deep place inside, allow your judgments and your opinions to drop away. Simply become the watcher. And feel the peacefulness that comes from letting go, from beginning to let go and dropping back into the witness. Feeling the peacefulness that comes from dropping back into the witness. Watching closely.

And as you step back and watch, you can also watch your mind as it spins its thoughts one after another, watching the mind with all its complexities, its preoccupations, its worries. Just becoming a witness to the mind. Watching your thoughts, no need to do anything, simply witnessing.

And as the breath settles you into the place of the witness, you can begin to detach from the intense drama of your life – seeing it, feeling it, but now, just watching it. Realizing that your life is unfolding just as it is meant to, no need to interfere, just watch. And as you drop back into the witness, you can feel the serenity of this detachment, the relaxation deep in your being. Whatever comes to the mind, just watch. If you notice that you are judging in any way, allow yourself to watch even the judgments. You are simply watching the judging mind. You can step back from the turmoil and busyness of your life, stepping off the track.

By falling back into your inner witness, you can find immense strength to deal with difficult times. Finding a place where you can just breathe and watch without having to do anything. Watching and staying centered. Centered and poised, allowing you to deal with situations staying very calm. Thoughts come, feelings come and you are just watching. This place, the place of our inner witness, is inside each one of us just waiting to be discovered.

Taking the time to slow down and relax. Taking the time to disengage from the flurry of life, from the compulsion of your thoughts. Not taking them so seriously, not taking anything so seriously. Taking time to step back and relax, taking time to stop our incessant doing and simply watching, allowing. Being in the moment, right here, right now. Settling into each breath, each moment. Very simple.

Now, allow your attention to return to the breath. Watching the breath coming and going, watching the belly rise and fall with each breath. Rising on the inhale, falling on the exhale. Slowly coming back to the body. Feeling the body. Coming back, very slowly and gradually. Taking a deep breath – being back fully alert and awake.

Meditation: Returning to the Belly

Close your eyes. Allow yourself to become comfortable so that your arms and legs are relaxed and comfortable. Now, gently go inside and just begin to relax into your breath, watching the inhale and the exhale. As you settle into the breath, feel the gentle rising and falling of your belly. Rising on the inhale, falling on the exhale. Slowly and gently, inhale, exhale, rising and falling. Very relaxed, very easy.

Very, very gently and slowly, allow your focus to come to your belly, feeling your belly, feeling the rising and the falling, feeling your breath as it comes in and going out, feeling the belly.

And as you focus on the belly, feeling the belly, see if you can just allow a spaciousness in your belly. Imagining the belly like a big bowl that is very spacious, very relaxed. Giving space, space to all the feelings, all the thoughts, all the sensations that come with total acceptance. No judgment, just acceptance.

Allow yourself to visualize this big bowl in your belly – a place where you can contain all the feelings. This bowl is big enough to contain every feeling that arises. A place to hold the feelings and watch them. No matter how strong the feelings, you can hold them right here in the belly. Allowing, without judgment.

Now visualize a candle flame in the center of your belly, burning very strongly and very steadily. Imagine that all around this candle flame there can be hurricanes of emotions, thoughts, chaos of all kinds, but nothing can disturb this flame. It continues to burn just as strongly, just as brightly no matter what is happening outside. Nothing touches it. Let yourself feel the intensity of this flame, the steadiness of this flame.

Our center is like this candle flame, our watcher is like this candle flame. It watches, it feels, it allows, but stays calm and relaxed. No judgment, no need to react, no need to panic. Just watching, feeling, allowing. Centered, relaxed, calm, composed. This place is in all of us just waiting to be uncovered, just waiting to be discovered.

And now, taking a deep breath, allowing yourself, very gently to come back. Coming back slowly, and opening your eyes.

******

Part 5

Relating Beyond Fear -
The Road to Conscious Love

Chapter 16

The Labyrinth of Projection

The basis of our conflicts and difficulties in relating is fear and its close cousin, insecurity. Once we begin to understand, accept and feel the fear, we also pave the way for relating in a totally new way – with consciousness instead of reaction. In the last section of this journey, we take the exploration of our fears into the arena of relating and finding ways to relate beyond the fear. Our wounds occurred from others. Unfortunately, we can't heal our fear and our mistrust by hugging a tree. We weren't abused by a tree. We have to rebuild our trust where it was damaged – with people.

Our relating is dominated by fear. We cover this fear with projections. Understanding projection is an essential part of our journey out of fear and co-dependency.

When we are in a projection with someone, we are not with ourselves and we are not in our center. We have given our power away to that person. To get that power back and to find our center, we have to unravel the projection. It is as if the person we are projecting on holds a piece of us that we have to reclaim by dealing with the projection. To do that, we have to identify the fear that is behind each projection.

We Project Our Need to Be Parented

Our wounded child is a projecting machine. The basis of most of these projections is to get the parenting we never had. It can come out in all kinds of different ways - demanding, idolizing, pleasing, rebelling - all reactions to the parent that our wounded child hungers for. We do it with lovers, friends and authority figures, usually unconsciously, and cover it up with all our compensations. After all, we think we are adult and don't have these unresolved, immature issues. But it is precisely our significant relationships that can help us to get in touch with all

187

the unconscious projecting that we do and they force us to look at them.

Deep down, there is such a deep longing in our child to be seen, loved and supported and not controlled, ignored or manipulated. That need in itself is not the problem. The problem is how we deal with it. One of the beauties and paradoxes of intimacy is that we can actually get the parenting we need, but only once we recognize our projections. We already know that because of the unmet needs of our inner child, we expect. *To meet these expectations, we unconsciously regress into a needy, or clinging, or demanding, or reacting child.* In that expecting regressed space, we project our longing and hunger on anyone who fits the bill. Our hungry child projects onto a friend or lover, the parent we never had. He or she doesn't like that so much and pushes us away.

When these unconscious mechanisms are in operation, both people in any relationship easily feel hurt and retreat into their fear and defenses. Trust is gone and the love cannot survive. We all do it. How to get the parenting we so desperately need and give ourselves and the other the freedom and respect that we all also so desperately need? We want to give love and we want to give the other the space he or she needs.

But before that can happen, we have to understand more precisely how the other person triggers our unhealed wounds from the past, provoking our defenses, our fears, and our hurts and disappointments. By becoming aware of our projections, we actually come to parent our own child because we begin to take responsibility for our needs rather than unconsciously expecting another person to take care of them. Let's investigate some important ways that our needs for parenting get projected.

Repeating Old Patterns

The first way to start is simply to begin to identify our repetitive patterns in relationships. Long ago, Freud discovered that we have a compelling drive to reenact the relating patterns of our earliest relationships, especially those with our parents, in later significant connections. He called it, "The repetition compulsion." We will replicate all of our dominant childhood relationships because we need to complete what was left uncompleted in those situations. We need to master our unfinished lessons.

This is most obvious in a love relationship where we are in some way finishing what was left unhealed with one or both of our parents, particularly our opposite sex parent. We will attract persons who for one reason or another bring up the wounds that came from that relationship. The wound is basically some form of incomplete or inadequate parenting. This phenomenon also arises with authority figures. Why? Because we want to get from them the support and guidance we never got as a child. Instead, what we attract often is more control and repression. Then we either rebel or collapse.

I learned something of my own patterns with women by trying to understand and feel as deeply as I could my own relationship with my mother. I came to see in my own primal work that I was fused with my mother and because of that, in all my later deep relationships with women, I have been afraid, better to say terrified, of either melting or separating. My mother, unknowingly and with the best of intentions, was smothering. She always did what she does best; she mothers. Intelligent, intuitive, strong and usually convinced that she is right about things, she was definitely a powerful force. I've been breaking out ever since, over and over again, one woman after another.

I remember a small incident when I was twenty-two. I was going to hike up Mt. Sinai as part of a guided tour of the Sinai desert. My parents were living in Israel then and Israel had just captured the Sinai desert. She suggested I take tennis shoes. I took sandals. All the way up the mountain, I regretted not taking those tennis shoes. Again, my mother was right. But it was a simple choice; either get bloody feet or feel castrated. I chose bloody feet.

Naturally, my girlfriends have always been strong, intelligent and potentially overpowering women. For some time, I just reacted to

189

the power trips with either shock or rebellion or some confused mixture of both. And I blamed at every opportunity I got. It never even occurred to me that I was creating these experiences to learn something. But I was simply reenacting my castration wound. From participating in and leading men's workshops, I have found that all men, one way or another, have to deal with their relationship with their personal mother and with the universal mother. Intensively. And one of the comforting things about working with other men is discovering that I am not alone. Each man has his own unique castration wound from his mother and recreates it in his intimate relationships with women.

Most men I have known are terrified at a deep and unconscious level of opening to a woman and find all kinds of ways to avoid it. They may become collapsed, abusive or withdrawing, but it is just variations of the same wound. Because some part of us desperately wants a mother, to become vulnerable with a woman is inviting castration. And that is terrifying. It is one of the great Zen koans for all men. To avoid the fears, we'll do anything that gives us the illusion of power and control. To be able to open deeply to a woman, we have to find our real strength and power; both the strength of being able to stand alone and the courage to dive deeply into a woman.

Women also reenact their abuse story with their father, often finding themselves attracted and involved with a man who has a tendency, overtly or covertly, to treat them in ways that are similar to how their father treated them. Often this takes the form of reenacting the pain of their victimization and helplessly suffering the abuse repeatedly. Or becoming a dutiful caretaker. Or playing the role of a tyrant and taking revenge for a passive, unavailable and ineffectual father.

We Can Stop the Patterns by Becoming Aware of Our Fears

Once we identify the patterns, the next question is, how to stop them from reoccurring? This question comes up in our work more than any other. The destructive patterns come from our wounds. One way to stop the repetition is to explore our relationship with our opposite sex parent as intimately, as energetically and intensively as possible. Without awareness and understanding, our patterns remain masochistic or abusive. But if we understand why we are doing it and energetically connect with the shame inside and our fears of abandonment, we can transform the pattern instead of perpetuating our suffering. We have lessons to learn. And relationship is surely one of the main ways that we learn them.

We have no choice but to repeat these patterns until we have learned whatever lesson we need to learn. We have to learn these lessons energetically, not just intellectually – feeling the shame and the shock. As much as we may berate ourselves for not finding something that appears more harmonious, more flowing and less conflictual, we are setting it up exactly as we want to and need to. Our higher consciousness knows that we are here for growth and will create those situations that inspire it.

Splitting into Good Parent and Bad Parent

The projection story gets more complicated. Not only does it determine who we attract, it also runs how we relate once we are in relationship. From the perspective of our wounded child, we see in the other one of two things – good parent or bad parent. Our wounded child wants and needs to feel loved and supported. When he gets that from the other, he sees good-loving parent. When he doesn't, he sees rejecting-bad parent.

For me, good mother is warm, juicy and loving, intuitively understanding and supportive, regards her spiritual path and meditation as the most important focus in life, but also is able to be totally present for me (not always but often), feels and shares her feelings with me, is also able to give me plenty of space and time to be alone and is devoted and committed to me. When she isn't showing me these qualities, she turns into bad mother. When good mother is there, I am happy. When bad mother is there, I am angry, depressed and moody.

Obviously, no one can meet our wounded child's needs for good parent. But that doesn't stop us from trying. Our rational adult may know that it is not possible, but not our child. So, when our wounded child doesn't get good parent, he or she acts out – by throwing tantrums, pouting, retreating, crying, pretending we don't care, taking revenge and so on. And this reaction can be triggered simply with a misunderstanding, a comment, a distraction of our lover's energy into something else; the smallest thing that makes us feel unloved. Then the good parent has become the rejecting parent. The sun has gone behind the clouds. And we may have little or no idea why or even that we are doing all this. Our child has little interest or understanding for complexity and is also not tuned in to the needs of our lover or friend. The other person, feeling this projection, naturally doesn't feel much space. But in his or her own way, he is doing the same thing. Is it any wonder that our honeymoons end?

From my psychiatry training, I thought that this kind of "splitting", as it is called, was something common to people with severe personality disorders and severe childhood trauma. Imagine my surprise when I saw myself doing the same thing. Not once, but all the time. And not just with my lover, also with my close friends. One minute I am feeling in total harmony and the next, I am feeling abandoned and betrayed. As John Bradshaw describes in *Creating Love*, once we are in this regressed hurt child space, we hear and see things that weren't said or which aren't happening and we don't hear things that are said, or don't see things that are happening. We are lost in our hurt movie and from that perspective, we cannot experience reality.

Some years ago, I was working with a woman who was a combination of therapist, mentor and mother figure for me. She was a powerful influence in my life. At a certain point, however, I felt that she had stopped tracking me and I began to feel unseen and unsupported. I also felt that some of her own issues were contaminating her work with me. I felt abandoned and from that hurt and angry space, acted out by pushing her out of my life and becoming critical of her.

In retrospect, I see it very differently. In the eyes of my hurt child inside, she had gone from good parent to bad parent. Now, I can see that it was time for me to break away and move on alone, but the separation was very painful. Rather than feel the pain, I made her wrong. I put her into my bad parent projection. I find that this kind of projecting, this kind of splitting, is quite universal. The art is to catch it and be able to step back a bit, being aware of our hurt child and to know what is causing him or her to feel abandoned.

Rebelling

The plot thickens. Our wounded child is not only looking for a perfect parent and once having found a likely suspect, keeps splitting him or her between good and bad parent. We also want to *rebel against the parent*. We want to push against his or her love. It's a way of testing, of seeing if she (or he) really loves us, if she can handle us when we are not being nice, agreeable and conforming. Setting limits firmly but lovingly is a big and important part of good parenting and many of us never got that. So we hunger for it. We want to find out if someone loves us enough to handle us because it was too costly to rebel as a child.

Now, in our relationships, sometimes we play the good and obedient child, adapting and compromising to secure our lover's (the parent's) love. Then we get fed up with this role and turn into the rebellious and reactive child. Once we think that we have se-cured the love, then it becomes safe to test it and to play the rebel that we didn't dare play earlier. This situation comes up with lo-vers, friends and particularly with authority figures. One reason we create authority figures in our life is to rebel against them, rebelling against the rules they set, the restrictions they impose and the advice they give. We seek out guidance and structure and then we rebel against it. We want support and approval from authority figures and then find fault with their guidance for not being perfect.

Even though the person we project on may or may not be like our original parent, in the mind of our child, we are sure he or she is.

In the past, in situations where I projected on authority figures, I could feel the conflicting feelings inside. One part of me wanted to surrender and to be open to being taught and receiving guidance and another part of me was always on guard not to be controlled or held back. It is a deep wound. The minute I felt that my energy was being restricted unjustly, I freaked out. It was an ongoing process of learning to take the power back by trusting myself. But the more I trusted myself, the less I had to give my power away. Now, I find that I can still be open and receive guidance, but I don't give myself away any longer.

Bonding Patterns

Very often in a long term relationship, we get crystallized into roles. This is what Hal Stone, in his book *Embracing Each Other* has called a "bonding pattern". There are different kinds of bonding patterns, but the most common is a bonding between parent and child. In these roles, we get lost in a projection. In the child role, as I have said, we see the lover as a parent who is often similar in significant ways to our original parents. In the parent role, we assume often the characteristics of one or both of our parents and react to our lover as our parents reacted to us as a child. It is also the way that we react to our own inner child.

Most relationships become bonded. It is natural because once the honeymoon is over, our unresolved fears and insecurities make us neurotically dependent on each other. But the beauty of bonding is that it can make us aware of our unresolved stuff. Whatever is unfinished and unworked through will surface in our relationships in the form of these bonding patterns. However, a bonding pattern that is not identified and worked through is death to the love and the aliveness in any relationship. The paradox is that often, unless we bond, we cannot move through what we need to. We have to bond because the bonding brings the hurt and needs to the surface. Also, for a time, the kind of security that bonding provides may be exactly what our wounded child needs. I suspect we have all been in a bonded situation. And because the needs of our wounded child are so great and so hidden, most long-term relationships become bonded.

But there are problems with bonding. We have to bring awareness to it. The security kills the energy and often sexuality is the first aspect that suffers. Parents and children don't make for good lovers. The parent becomes resentful that he or she seems to be doing all the giving and the child gets resentful because he or she feels dependent and patronized. Sooner or later one of them is sure to rock the boat. One person will inevitably break the bonding because, deep down, a bonded situation is not truthful and not alive. The parent hides behind the role to feel more in control and to gratify his or her self-image. He doesn't want to show – to himself or to others – that he too is needy and wounded. He is simply too frightened to admit that he also needs to be parented and covers up the vulnerability by playing the parent role. The child hides by playing the child and not wanting to grow up and take responsibility for his or her life. As soon as one recognizes the situation, he or she will move one way or another to break the pattern by finding another lover, moving out or creating conflict.

Our love affairs (and close friendships) are no longer a parent-child situation – they are a friend-to-friend situation. With awareness, we can take turns parenting each other and exposing and sharing our child to each other. When we bring consciousness to these roles, our parent side becomes naturally nurturing or limit setting in a way that is gentle and centered. On the child side, we can also honor and express our vulnerability and rebelliousness and playfulness in an equally centered and gentle way, doing it in a way that brings us closer together.

Taking Revenge

Now we come to the dark knight (and night) in the projecting game – the place inside us where we are waiting to take revenge. Somebody said once that relationships were 90% about revenge. I think that's a bit exaggerated, but we need to be mindful of this tendency. The amount of energy we hold inside in resentment and unexpressed rage from our childhood is great and often we don't become aware of it until it surfaces in our relationships. Because

195

we repressed the rage from being humiliated, abused and betrayed as a child, we walk around unconsciously with a packet of Tomahawk missiles inside waiting to be launched!

Our lover or anyone who triggers this wound becomes the target of all that repressed energy. In a recent individual session I did, a man talked about how he was not able to get close to a woman. The smallest thing would make him angry and he would react vehemently at the slightest criticism. Exploring more deeply, we discovered that his mother had been overbearing and had deeply shamed his sexuality with her repressive Catholic conditioning.

We were much too disempowered, too shocked and too compromised as a child to express or even feel any of these feelings. In our current relationships, it usually takes some time for the projection to surface, but sooner or later, it will. Then, the other person becomes some complex mix of our internalized parent and the actual person. He or she gets confused with those who inflicted our wounds from the past. But at last, we have an opportunity to get revenge. All this rage inside begins to come out in ways that can be deadly, in verbal or physical abuse, in teasing, being sarcastic, patronizing, matronizing, cutting off, comparing or making love with others, making our lover feel inadequate sexually and so on.

We can work to heal our energy of revenge only if we are aware that it is there. I have found that by exploring the direct and indirect ways that my anger comes out is one of the major ways that I can access my repressed anger. My pattern is to retreat in shock when I have felt hurt. Then I take revenge and punish, mostly by cutting off and withholding my energy, or by making snide comments. Yuk! Often, I don't even know that I am doing it. But from working on it, I can feel the energy of revenge more and more. It is very deep, but when it is triggered it almost feels endless. Yet, once I can express the energy, it changes.

Each one of us has his or her own way of expressing revenge and of leaking out all our repressed resentments for past injuries. In a session with a couple, a woman complained that she felt put down by her boyfriend's teasing. He was totally unaware that he was doing anything abusive. He thought that his teasing was all in fun. It was a complete surprise to him that she felt disturbed by it. In another case, a man I was working with felt extremely wary of any woman trying to control, dominate or overprotect him. He noticed that his bond with his mother was extremely tight and on a deep level felt a fusion of boundaries between them. His mother was powerful and controlling and instead of encouraging his independence, kept him subtly bonded to her. He did not feel the space to develop confidence in himself, or to make his own mistakes. Now he finds himself attracted to lovers who are also powerful and potentially controlling. Whenever he feels manipulation or control, he collapses and goes into shock. When he recovers from the shock, which is taking less and less time as he works on his inner feelings, he begins to reconnect more with his rage inside and he reacts impetuously and irrationally to even the suspicion of control or manipulation. Sometimes he can distinguish between lover and mother, but often, particularly when the wounds have been triggered, he can't.

Projecting Unlived Parts of Ourselves on Others

There is another important piece to the projection story, another way of understanding the complexity of our projections. *We also project onto others and particularly our lovers, parts of ourselves that are inside, but are unlived.* In his book Hal Stone calls these "disowned selves". This projection has the potential to be either an intense source of growth or trouble depending on how much awareness and understanding we approach it with. Our conscious self is only a small part of our consciousness. One of the most significant ways that we discover parts of ourselves that are hidden is by attracting lovers and friends who are living those aspects.

When I was in high school, I fell in "love", (it would be more accurate to say that I fell in fascination) with a girl in the class behind me. She was everything that I wasn't – wild, crazy and unpredictable. I was focused on academics and sports and on getting into an Ivy League college. She could have cared less. She was interested in acting and art and she was not ruled by conformity or conventional approval. On the contrary, she rebelled against all this conditioning. This rebellion, together with her aliveness and beauty captured me and fascinated me. I pursued her for nearly two years without much success and my heart pined. Every unrequited love song I heard felt as if it was about me. Years later, I again fell desperately in love with another wild and crazy artist. The projection of these unlived parts of myself was still operating. My conditioning had brought out the highly responsible, ordered and disciplined sides at the expense of my wildness.

We are both attracted to and repelled by the parts of ourselves we see reflected in others. That is what makes up our likes and dislikes. We are attracted because we want to rediscover our unlived parts and repelled because our conditioning has taught us to reject these parts. I could recognize this split whenever I was with someone who I felt was much more wild, spontaneous and free than I experienced myself to be. One side of me was totally drawn to this energy; another judged it as irresponsible – wild one vs. responsible one.

A friend of mine has a relationship with a very emotional, at times hysterical woman. She is much more in touch with her feelings than he is, but she also uses her emotions to manipulate him. Just like his mother did. He responds by avoiding his feelings and turning her off whenever she gets emotional. Naturally, this enrages her. He is not seeing that she is carrying the projection of his emotional nature. He sees feelings as ways that he gets manipulated, by his mother as a child and now by his girlfriend. But by using the ostrich approach, he does not heal his wound. While we have worked together, he has begun to rediscover his own emotional nature, owning back the projection. As he finds his own way of feeling and expressing emotions, he is less susceptible to being manipulated with them.

I noticed that until I was able to connect with my vulnerable child, I judged others for their vulnerability by considering it a weakness. In my first long-term relationship, I could not see that my lover's emotions, depressions and fears were mirroring my own inner child whom I was not connected with. I judged her for being so "moody", "heavy" and fixated on her feelings. In fact, she was my first real teacher of the heart. But I didn't know it then. Over the years, I have been exploring my inner female and I have been amazed at how incredibly shy and insecure she is. I never realized just how sensitive and hidden I was. I had so judged and so, pushing male, that it didn't have the space to come out.

I have since recognized how devalued the feminine was in my family and with it all the values of the feminine – receptivity, intuition, irrationality and especially feeling and expressing emotions. Since then, I have communicated with my feminine part much more. I meet her in the moments when I am quiet and meditating or when listening to my spiritual master. And I recognize her in my lover. I have also recognized that my deepest piece of work in rediscovering my maleness has come from learning to appreciate the feminine again.

Each of the major relationships I have been in has reflected parts of me that I was not in touch with. But I seldom had enough understanding of the projection to see what I was doing. Because so much of our inner child is buried in the unconscious, it is difficult to see how much the people we are with intimately actually have a child inside who is very similar to our own. The other person, by being our mirror, gives us an opportunity to recognize the needs, the hunger, the fears and the strength, the wildness and the sensitivity of our inner child that we have buried under our protection. What we reject or admire in them is what we reject and repress in ourselves. Understanding this projection becomes a way that we can reclaim those lost parts of ourselves. Without this understanding, it usually becomes a nightmare of blame and conflict.

In our projections, we often are acting out an ongoing inner war *between our fear and sense of freedom.* We judge others for the freedom that we would like to take but are too afraid. I am embarrassed to admit how many of my judgments of others are based on this projection. When I am lost in a judgment, I have to bring myself back, remind myself that projection is going on and take a look at what I am repressing at that moment. Instead of sticking to the roles that are familiar and safe and attacking others for what my narrow-mindedness cannot relate to, I can begin to use the other to expand.

Learning to Distinguish the Trigger from the Source

Our projections cover up much of the fear we are holding inside that we will not get what we need. The person who is the object of our projection usually triggers our fears (and expectations) of being betrayed, controlled, misunderstood, abused or abandoned. Just recall the last time you felt hurt by someone. Didn't this person bring up these fears and in a way that has happened many times before in your life? Our relationships are highly loaded situations. We are bringing much more to them than it seems. Why? Because we are searching for the perfect parent and we get disappointed over and over again. But we are usually unaware of the intensity of the feelings that we repressed until the wound becomes triggered.

A projection is a reenactment of the past. A big part of our healing comes when we begin to be able to distinguish the trigger from the source. When a person provokes one of our wounds, it seems absolutely that he (or she) is the one who is causing the pain. He is the problem, not the parent or sib or teacher or classmate who hurt us so many years ago. Often our projection is provoked because the person now in our life shares some of the characteristics of the person who hurt us originally.

Our reaction is out of proportion to the stimulus. We enter every relationship already sensitive to being treated how we were treated as a child. I can see in myself that as soon as I feel controlled, I react. I don't see the reality; I see every person who has ever tried to control me. My emotional charge is fueled with the belief formed by my childhood experience that no one really understands me. The art is not to get lost in the projection. Maybe we are being controlled, abused, abandoned, or perhaps we

200

imagine it. Perhaps it is a bit of both. The other person feels gripped by our projection. They feel not seen for who they are and get angry or pull away.

Of course, there are no innocent victims in this game. It always takes two to play. We are locked in each other's projections whether with lovers, friends or people in authority. They too have their part. But once both people in any relationship can identify the patterns and start to take some responsibility for their own part in the drama, healing happens. Then we can begin to take responsibility for the feelings rather than blaming the other for the anger or pain that is coming up.

We Have to Keep Investigating Our Denial

If something is blocking our heart, often what is in the way is an unconscious projection from one or both sides that hasn't been revealed and talked about. Often our anger, hurt and feelings of betrayal with other people come from our needs and wants, many of which we have repressed and denied. We keep our projection unconscious because we don't want to admit and accept just how needy our child inside really is. This neediness goes against what we think is acceptable, attractive or spiritual.

Carla, for instance, has the unconscious projection on her lover that he will provide for her and take care of her. This attitude runs contrary to her conscious idea of how she wants to be with a man – independent and self-reliant. But her child inside was not around when she formed these beliefs. Her child wants to be taken care of. Confronted with her desire to be provided for, she would deny it. When her lovers fall short of her expectation to be treated as a princess, she gets very angry. With work on bringing these projections to awareness, she has uncovered the pain that she is holding inside, never having had a father who gave her the comfort and security that she needed as a child. Allowing the pain has helped her to react differently when her expectations in her current relationship are not met. She feels and shares the pain that is triggered instead of casting blame on her lover.

Stephen is a seminar leader, very charismatic and skilled. But he can't see that underneath his image is a desperately hungry and lonely child longing for love. He continues to hide these needs behind his success as a group therapist, moving from one brief romance to another. He just can't see what he is denying. To get in touch with these needs, he would have to drop under the image and into his wounded inner child.

To penetrate our denial and come to accept our needs, it is helpful to ask ourselves what we are really looking for. What is our perfect parent like?

Here are a few questions that might help:

- How do we know when we feel safe, loved, felt and supported?
- When do we feel that the other person is holding us in their heart and there is space for us?
- And, how does it feel when we are doing the same for the other?

Charles came for help because his girlfriend of two years was cutting off from him. She complained that he wasn't open enough and she was getting tired of trying to connect. Five years ago, he had been deeply in love with another woman who left him for another man. He decided that he would never become so needy again, retreated into his music and slowly put himself back together. But the wound was still there and he was still much too afraid to open. He felt sure that if he showed his new lover how needy he was, she would certainly reject him just as the other had. Our needs don't go away even if we put up a pretense of strength. If we can embrace our needy child, beginning to feel and accept the hunger, fear and pain inside, we come back to ourselves again and, in the bargain, get love from others.

From Projection to Wholeness

We all project. Whether we can grow from it or allow it to take us deeper into misery and drama has to do with how much we understand about what we are doing. Either we become fossilized into projection patterns, or we use the projection to learn continuously more about ourselves.

Projection can be either fertile territory for self-exploration and growth or conflict and stagnation. My master once said that when we understand about our projections, relationships develop into a sharing of our silence. It seems a long way away! But then again, who knows? Right now, all we can do is compassionately develop more and more understanding about them.

Exercise 1: Identifying Repetitive Patterns

Take a moment to investigate your most significant relationships, starting with your love affairs. Perhaps the following questions will be helpful. You might want to write down the answers as you go along.

When you review these relationships, the one you are in now (if you are involved at present) and those of the past, do you notice that you have been treated in a similar way?

- In what ways have you allowed yourself to be abused, mistreated, or misunderstood?

- In what ways have you compromised yourself?

- In what ways have you been the one who was abusive and is there a familiar pattern here as well?

- Have your lovers given you the same feedback over and over again? And do you react in the same way each time?

- Is there a pattern in how you protect yourself?

- What are the common negative beliefs about love and opening, which are re-affirmed over and over again?

Continuing with the exercise, scan the most significant relationships that you are involved in at present: your closest friendships, your relationship with your boss and your children. Do you notice any similarity between these and relationships from your childhood?

For instance:

- With close friendships, is there something that reminds you of a relationship with a sibling?

- With authority figures, is there something that reminds you of your relationship with your father or sibling?

- With your children, do you see any similarity between how you are with them to how your parents were with you?

Notice the similarities and write them down. Perhaps without being aware of it, you have created these relationships in your life in order to complete something. Often, those that seem the most difficult and which we would like to be rid of are actually the ones from which we have most to learn. Take a moment with each of these relationships to see if you can discern what the lesson might be.

Exercise 2: Discovering Your Internalized Parent

Sit facing two cushions – one on the right and one on the left. Allow one cushion to represent your internalized parent and the other your vulnerable child. Allow yourself to come seated on the parent cushion facing the child and begin to talk to the child. Then, in time, go to the child cushion and respond. Continue to go back and forth allowing the space to deepen, noticing what surfaces. What does the parent say to the child? What is the energy that he or she places on the child? How does the child respond? And what happens to the energy of the child?

Exercise 3: Identifying Unlived Parts of Yourself

On a clean piece of paper, write a list of:

- The characteristics in people that you like the most
- The characteristics in people that you dislike the most

When you surround yourself with people who have the first qualities, it probably makes you feel at home, nourished and loved. Some of these may be qualities that you have, but are not living as much as you like.

When you attract people who have the second qualities, it gives you a chance to look at parts of yourself that you don't want to look at. Now,

- Make a list of what attracts you to lovers
- Make a list of what qualities you find in your lovers

Compare these two lists. Those items that are the same may be unlived parts of yourself that you find attractive and those that are only on the second list, but not on the first, may be unexplored parts of yourself that you judge.

******

Chapter 17

Respect & Boundaries
Part I - Respecting Ourselves

Opening brings fear. One of the biggest fears, and one that we have all certainly experienced, is that when we open, we will be invaded, abused or in some way taken advantage of. We want to open, but we don't want to be hurt. If we remain in our closed, protected and isolated world, we can at least try to not get hurt. But that doesn't work anymore, particularly not at this stage in our journey. So what to do? I have found that this issue opens a door to a very important aspect of our work with ourselves. When we come out of isolation and recognize that it is part of our healing to learn to relate, one of our tasks is to learn respect – respect for ourselves and for others. It is difficult because of our conflicting desires that cause us to bump against each other. How to create a world for ourselves where we can meet our needs and respect those of the people close to us? I think this is one of the main lessons we all have to learn, over and over again.

Two Sides of Entitlement

The issue of respect provokes two different energies inside each of us. One operates under the feeling that unless I seize what I want, I will not get it. The other is deeply shocked, has not the ability and confidence to say "No" and believes that everyone is always taking advantage of me. One says, "Don't repress me. I want to move my energy!" and "I want what I want and I want it now!" The other is saying, "Please don't leave me. I'll give you whatever you want." Then gets resentful and feels that, "It is not safe to trust anyone."

The first carries the belief that everyone is trying to suppress our energy and hold us down. The second believes that no one respects our space and our integrity. It may not seem that we have both of these voices inside because we may have suppressed one of them. But we do. However, at any given moment, we may be

207

identifying with one and our lover or friend with the other. They are two unhealed wounds demanding to be worked through. They also, I suspect, bring up unlearned karmic lessons that we have to work through – one to learn to respect others' needs and the other to learn to respect our own.

We do not respect each other. Why? Because our survival needs blind us. If we all lived our Buddha nature, living totally conscious lives, we could exist in the world in a perfectly innocent, vulnerable and open state. Unfortunately, the world isn't like that, at least not yet. Convinced that to survive, we have to take care of and protect ourselves, we are often less than sensitive to each other. We invade each other's space. Our boundaries were not respected as a child. So, naturally we lost the ability to respect them – ours or anyone else's. Both can be totally unconscious.

Here's an example: Some years ago, a friend borrowed my portable stereo without asking. I came home and noticed that it was gone – no note, nothing. I couldn't understand what happened to it. I naturally assumed that I had lost it or someone stole it. A few days later, my friend mentioned to me, "Oh, by the way, I borrowed your stereo for a few days. I'll bring it back tomorrow, okay?" Relieved that I discovered where it went, and because I am such a "nice" person, I answered, "Oh, sure, no problem." I immediately told myself that I shouldn't be so picky to be disturbed by someone borrowing something from me, especially such a close friend. But I felt unsettled inside and the next time I saw my friend, I felt distant from him.

We take both sides of this drama; either the one who is invaded or the one who invades. We need to learn how to set our limits assertively and gracefully and we need to learn how to be sensitive to another's need and space while still being sensitive to our own. Let's explore each of these two areas.

The Healing of the Solar Plexus

We gain self-respect when we learn to love ourselves and feel ourselves enough to honor our preciousness. When we rediscover our preciousness, we naturally honor our boundaries and we find the skill and the courage to protect our own space. Prior to that, we rotate between victim and tyrant. The victim puts out an energy that invites shame and the tyrant shames to avoid feeling his own shame. Before doing co-dependency work, I had no accurate understanding for boundaries – mine or anyone else's. I allowed myself to be invaded without understanding what was happening and I invaded others' space without much sensitivity. I just thought I was being a nice and generous person. Of course, I couldn't explain the resentments or the humiliating feelings that were inside.

From the victim side, I rarely even recognized that I was being invaded. In those moments when I did recognize feeling disturbed by what someone had done or said, I minimized it and pretended that I didn't really care. Or I would deny my hurt and explain it away intellectually. Any of these ways was easier than having to confront the person. "Oh, it's not such a big deal," I could now hear myself saying, or "I guess I need to learn to be more giving or more forgiving," or "Oh, they just did that because they didn't think."

Underneath our inability to set limits is the fear of losing the love of that person, or the fear that they could get angry with us, cut off or invalidate what we are saying. The voice says something like, "If I say how I feel or if I assert myself, I will be punished, invalidated, cut off, violated, aggressed upon, raged at, or abused." Because of our shame, we simply lost contact with our own feelings and with our own space. Our needs for love and approval were so desperate that we shrank our needs into taking a smaller and smaller space. We invite invasion because we are not living our energy. When invasion comes, we don't recognize it and we keep reinforcing the inner program that our boundaries are not important enough to be respected. *To the wounded child, self-respect seems far less important a priority than love.* Love

209

and attention are a matter of life and death; self-respect is a luxury.

But to our being, self-respect is our life blood. From my shamed self, I function automatically from a space of fear and guilt, not wanting to cause any waves or risk any negative response.

Once, at a men's workshop with Robert Bly, he mentioned the importance of saying, "Wait a minute!" inside when something happens that doesn't feel right. I loved that. I notice that my obsession to please or withdraw when I feel hurt is so strong, that it takes more than a "waiting a minute" to change the pattern. But just giving myself the space to feel and to check in has made a lot of difference. In my own process of reclaiming my self-respect, I have noticed precise steps that I have had to take. These are highly overlapping stages, but nonetheless I notice a definite progression from one to the next.

Stage 1: Recognizing When We Are Invaded and Revalidating Our Boundaries

I became regressed and a pleaser in situations that were frightening because of my shock; because of my fear of violence or confrontation, anger or disharmony. When I started working with my shame and shock, I began to notice precisely what it felt like just after I had been invaded. I would be enjoying a connection with someone but afterwards, I would feel terrible. Then I would have to trace back to the time that I felt I had given myself away. I was too addicted to harmony to notice it at the time.

We blame others for shaming us, but it is not the other person's problem. It is our lesson to learn self-respect.

I can remember so many times in my life being shamed and not being able to say anything. Because of my fear and need for approval, I was sending out a vibration that invited humiliation and disrespect. By recognizing that I was setting it up with my nonverbal message, I began to penetrate my own shame.

210

The first step was simply learning to recognize when I had allowed myself to be shamed. That required learning and validating the space of shame and shock – feeling it in the body and feeling what it did to my energy, how it made me feel inside and how it made me feel about myself. In short, I needed to learn to recognize the attack.

Part of recognizing when I felt shamed or attacked required learning what boundaries are. It was a surprise for me to realize that such things as not listening when someone is talking to us, not honoring our agreements with each other, keeping someone waiting, not paying our debts without being reminded, taking something from someone without asking; all of these are boundary invasions. If we had little physical space of our own as a child, we may constantly feel closed in or simply adjust to denying ourselves. If we were sexually abused in any way as a child, relearning and validating our sexual boundaries is a monumental task. If we were emotionally abused by being taught to feel guilty for another's feelings, or by being told what we felt or thought, we will continually feel guilty when we assert ourselves.

Relearning and respecting my boundaries has been an ongoing process of coming back to myself and trusting my belly. It knows when something doesn't feel right.

Stage 2: Feeling and Working with the Fire

If our ability to feel and to express anger is repressed, we are cut off from our strength and that causes us to collapse and sink into humiliation. After I began to recover from my shock, the rage that was lurking underneath began to surface. Learning to say no and bringing back self-respect means reconnecting with the rage our child holds inside for all the humiliation and invasion he or she received. In spite of whatever survival strategy we developed to deal with the assault to our integrity, our child inside did not forget a single insult. Where does all that resentment go? Inside – buried under guilt and fear. Then it leaks out in all kinds of indirect ways – by being passive aggressive, moody, bitchy,

211

complaining, sarcastic and violent. We will create situations that will trigger the rage to be awakened. Then it is up to us how creative we are in working with it once it has been provoked.

I recall an event in which this process unfolded in my own life. I was working in a therapy school as one of the principal therapists. The director and I respected each other a great deal but had a different approach to working with people – I was more psychologically oriented, his focus was more esoteric. At one point, he sent his girlfriend into one of my workshops ostensibly as an assistant but actually, he had a hidden agenda to create a more uniform presentation of the work in the school along the lines of his approach. At first, I welcomed it as a possibility to grow but soon recognized that his friend had little understanding for how I was working and was there to influence rather than support me. I felt totally violated and said so to my collegue. He apologized and admitted his unclarity immediately. On the surface, all seemed fine and resolved. But it wasn't resolved for me because the incident triggered a big wound inside.

I harbored anger and resentment. With time, I began to see that it touched my deep wound inside of feeling disregarded and not respected, covering years of repressed anger for similar times when I didn't validate myself and my creativity. I was angry with myself for all the times that I had not respected or stood up for myself and furious with those whom I felt did not see and respect me. This kind of triggering also happens in all our relationships and particularly with our love relationships. If lovers don't fight once in a while, something is being suppressed. We are certain to push each other's buttons and trigger our hurt spaces. We can maintain the harmony just so long before our hurts from past wounds start to surface. Thank God. Without the combustion, I think we would all die of boredom.

Our relationships provoke our anger because we need to bring this energy out of repression and reclaim it. But how to deal with the fire once it gets triggered? To heal our solar plexus from collapse, we need to feel that natural feeling of "NO!" whenever our boundaries are being violated. But how to do that without

212

having our relating degenerate into blame and abuse as it so often does? We do have to rekindle the charge – working with getting back in touch with the anger that was repressed. Ideally, we can create a safe and contained space to let it out. To reconnect with the energy, it doesn't matter whether we are screaming at someone or at a pillow. But, at least in my experience, in reality, when the anger gets triggered it comes out and probably we need to go through a period where we react and express the anger to the person who has triggered it. I know that I did. If I stopped to think about the "right" way to work with my anger, it went back into repression. Reacting has seemed to help me to feel it.

Stage 3: Coming Back to Our Center

However, we don't heal our shame and bring back our self-respect by reacting and yelling at those who trigger our anger. *We heal it by coming back to ourselves,* by graduating from the stage of reacting when we feel taken advantage of to just feeling and trusting ourselves. Graduating from defense to centeredness. In the first, we are basically just feeding an addiction to react and get angry and find reasons to stay protected. In the second, we are at home with ourselves enough to know what is right for us and the protection is no longer needed.

Recently, I did a session with a couple who had just completed a workshop and were coming to find a way to resolve their conflicts. They had no trouble expressing anger with each other. But it was hard for both of them to trust each other enough to show their hurt. In the session, we worked with finding ways that each of them could take off their war paint and feel the vulnerability underneath. At the source of our anger there is nearly always deep insight about what the anger is really about and much vulnerability and grief.

In other situations, the opposite is true; it is growthful for both people to take the risk to express anger with each other. Two friends of mine have been together for four years but, because of their conditioning, were both terrified of expressing or receiving anger. The anger and resentments built up, as they usually do with couples that have been together for a while. Instead of putting out these resentments directly, they took indirect revenge on each other. They would cut off sexually, become bitchy and moody, complain about the other to friends, but not with each other and so on. Once they found the courage to express their irritations and resentments directly, their relating improved considerably.

For those of us who repressed our anger out of fear and collapse, expressing anger directly becomes a shock remedy. As a child, if we expressed anger, we got rejection or punishment back. Now we can learn to express it and see that not only can we stand in the fire and not die, but the person may still be there. People often feel that once they reclaim their ability to get angry then they have healed their shame wound. I wish it were so easy. But from collapse to being able to receive and express anger is an exhilarating step. It doesn't mean that we have found our power again, but we're getting closer. It gives us the strength that we can defend ourselves, that we have the power to protect our vulnerability.

As a child, I was teased by my older brother. That experience of teasing left a wound of expecting to be teased. It would happen with friends who provoked my older brother projection. One friend with whom I did have such a projection had a habit of mimicking me when I would say certain things he found ridiculous. The first time, I didn't say anything. I was in shock. But staying with the feelings, I noticed that under my shock was fury; a volcano of fury connected to all the times that I had been teased as a child and not reacted. I worked with the anger alone, but when it happened again, I was able to express my feelings to my friend. He apologized and was grateful that I had confronted him with it because he could see that it was the way he had treated his younger brother as a child.

But at the end of the process of healing our solar plexus and rediscovering our preciousness and self-respect, we come to a point where we are able to be assertive, centered and powerful in a way that is not contaminated with projection and we can be vulnerable instead of reactive. Assertiveness and vulnerability are two different ingredients of setting limits from this healed space that are appropriate in different situations. Let's look at each.

Responding from a centered space is a natural outcome of clearly knowing what we want, need and feel. The purpose is not to hurt, put down, attack, blame or punish the other person, but to bring more consciousness to a situation and to respond from a space that comes directly out of our integrity and self-respect. When I am connected with centered assertiveness, the energy is located in my belly. I may or may not feel anger, but the anger is not clouding my clarity. Opportunities to learn centered assertiveness come up all the time both with friends, lovers, acquaintances and people we work with. These situations have been a continual test for me to affirm my dignity and self-respect, not allowing things to slide by, minimizing or denying their importance.

With our more intimate relationships, we can often move into vulnerability when we feel invaded or disrespected. There are moments, many moments when one or both of us are lost in our wounded child and being demanding, manipulative, regressed or vengeful and we cannot step out of the role. There is no space or consciousness at the moment to see or feel what we are doing.

The deepest empowerment and self-respect does not come until we can feel the hurt that lies underneath the anger and can express it.

Until then, there is always a tension inside and we may be basing our power on being able to say no. But this kind of strength is still based on reaction and mistrust. The real empowerment comes from a place of inner relaxation, from trusting again and allowing ourselves to be vulnerable even if there is no guarantee that we will be treated as we would like to be. Energetically, it means moving from the solar plexus where the anger, reaction, and protection live and into the belly and the heart where we can connect with our vulnerability and hurt.

Gradually, I begin to see how deep and how old this wound of feeling mistrust and disrespected is inside me. It still heals. And it can still be easily triggered whenever anyone in my life pushes the same button. The rage becomes accompanied with much sadness for that little boy who had so little self-confidence and trust in himself that he allowed himself to be invalidated, and tears for that little boy who had such a struggle to find and stand up for his self-expression. How to take all this back to the arena of setting a limit? Is it safe or even appropriate to share our hurt and vulnerability? With my lover and close friends, I communicate the best when I can say, "It hurts," or "It hurt me when you ... " We often take time to ask each other if the other one has space right now to listen while we share the hurt and say what we don't like.

Deepening our intimacy with a lover or a friend actually depends on being able to share this way, being able to set a limit from a soft and trusting space. We are all trying as best we can to bring greater love into our life and so much of that has to do with staying open and sharing, even if we have felt invaded and disrespected.

Not so long ago, I had some conflicts with two friends. I felt invaded and disrespected by broken agreements and feeling disregarded. In the past, I might have ignored these things, but that no longer works for me. At first, I was outraged and hurt and felt myself cutting off from both of them. My first way of dealing with the hurt has always been to shut down and shut the person out; my old way, my familiar reaction to feeling wounded, that part of me who says, "Forget them, I don't need them in my life anyway." But working with these two situations taught me some valuable lessons, lessons that perhaps we can all learn in dealing with our fears of setting limits and learning to claim back our dignity and integrity.

With one friend, I could see that it was important to keep putting out when something comes between us. There is an entitled part of me that does not want to have to do that, who expects that if someone says they love me, they will always be sensitive to me. It has been a way of avoiding responsibility. I expect others, particularly those close to me, to be sensitive, just and honest.

And when they aren't, I feel betrayed. Walking around with these expectations has been a way that I could stay regressed and childish. My child inside does not want to admit and face that the world is simply not always honest, just and sensitive.

Furthermore, I was (and still am to some extent) in a mystified state of hoping that people I opened to would not hurt me. Instead of seeing each person and situation for what it is, I have projected my hope and my entitlement onto it. And it has repeatedly run me into trouble. Not wanting to see clearly, I have entered into relationships with lovers and friends from the space of a regressed child who wanted to be treated fairly. When I have found the courage and the commitment to share my hurt, I usually feel understood and taken in. That happened in this case. I could use the incidents that triggered my hurt, see my own sensitivities and see my part of the story. But more importantly, it re-enforced something that I am continuing to learn – to continue to state clearly and repeatedly when something happens between me and another that doesn't feel right.

With the second person, it was more involved than just setting a limit. I had many unconscious expectations and projections that I was putting onto him that I was not in touch with. I was not aware how much he triggered a wound inside me of feeling not respected and inferior and I was too proud to admit it to him. I needed to get in touch with my projection, drop my pride and expose myself. Often, when we feel invaded by someone, there is also a deep wanting from the person that we are not in touch with. That wanting triggers the shame, but we are either too proud or too stubborn to see it. It is not enough just to set a limit because then we are not going to the root.

This situation arises frequently with parents. Most of us have to go through a period of setting limits with them one way or another. But we also have to get in touch with what we still want and expect from them. Setting a limit does little to heal the shame wound if we have not recognized the projection. A friend of mine gets outraged when her father criticizes her for how she earns her living. But she still takes money from him and, so naturally, he

217

has her power in this area. For years, I felt hurt when my father would not accept my alternative lifestyle and would make deprecating comments about it. Behind my hurt was an unrecognized desire that he accepts and respects me for the choices that I had made.

In these cases, our shame arises at least as much from not taking responsibility for our own life as it does from not knowing how to say no. I saw that my shame prevented me from seeing and feeling myself as a person who could deal with life. I did not feel the strength inside to see and deal with each situation for what it was and is. And so, I regressed and did not take full responsibility. This shame made me still want to be parented. But rather than recognize and work through all of this, I choose to feel betrayed when people were not as I expected them to be. In all of these cases, the important point is that our self respect does not depend on how or who we are with the other. It depends more on how we are with ourselves.

In this final stage of setting limits, there is the awareness that our connecting with others is not a fight but an opportunity to feel our own vulnerability. Once the solar plexus is healed, we don't have the need anymore to prove that we can defend our damaged child from further abuse. The charge is gone, the war is over and our responses are not contaminated with reactions from repressed resentments. If we feel invaded and there is space to share the hurt, we can share it. If there is no space, then we can use centered assertiveness.

The stages that I have described are an ongoing, overlapping process. Often, I still don't reach a point of being clear and nonreactive. I am still full of charge and anger inside. I get resentful, I cut off, I pout, I take revenge and punish. In short, I still do all the things that I wouldn't do if I were conscious. But I can watch all of it with a bit more distance. And rather than remain in shock and hidden resentment, I can feel and express. More often now, I am also able to express the hurt.

Feeling the energy and expressing the hurt seems to be a major source of bringing back our self-respect. Eventually, I find we come to a point where we can see that no one is taking advantage of us. Even that idea is still a product of our shame and shock. It's part of the trance. To come out of it, we have to feel ourselves differently – to feel our center and our dignity. It happens slowly and as it does, the paranoia and mistrust become less and less. As we heal, we become more able to say directly how we feel. The healing is dropping down out of the reaction, the protection and the attack into our vulnerability, going from the solar plexus to the belly.

A New Self-Image

I discovered from working on my shame that I was deeply identified with a self-image as a shamed person. I was someone who could and should be humiliated. Then it changed to someone who always had to stand up for himself so he won't be taken advantage of. But that was all part of the same victim, shamed identity. As long as I was living with a shamed self-image I was living my life in a way that didn't bring me self-respect and it fed my shame. Out of this shamed self-image, I was dishonest, avoided confrontation, did not honor my commitments to myself or to others, diluted my energy with distraction and addiction, or spaced out. Working with the shame, something changed. I stopped thinking of myself as a shamed person.

As long as our wounds of shame remain unhealed, we recreate our offenders as a repetition of earlier experience. They are not the problem. It is our narcissistic injury, the wound to our self-respect that is the problem. Our healing comes from connecting with the pain inside and eventually finding enough inner centeredness that the abuses stop happening. We stop the abusiveness from the outside by doing the inner work, by knowing and feeling the shame, by coming to feel ourselves more and more and by loving that wounded kid inside.

******

219

Chapter 18

Respect & Boundaries
Part II - Respecting Others

Most of us not only get invaded, but we also invade. It always seems to go both ways. I find that the area of respecting others and seeing how we unconsciously invade their boundaries is one of the places where we come up against our biggest blind spots. I think it is because our panic is so deep. Our survival panic gives us the feeling that we have to get our needs met at any cost. To be sensitive to the other's needs and space seems too threatening.

If confronted with our lack of sensitivity, our reactive-entitled child responds with, "Look, I have to move with my energy. I can't always be limiting myself. If you get angry or hurt, that's your responsibility." Or, we respond with complete denial, "What do you mean I was insensitive to you? I have no idea what you are talking about." Or we feel guilty.

Deep down, I think, we know our pockets of selfishness and the ways that we put our own needs first at the expense of others. Some of this is covered with denial, but much of it drifts into our awareness from time to time. Secretly, we may feel ashamed about our self-centeredness and abusiveness. But it doesn't change so easily.

I have found three aspects to my process of working on respect for others.

1) Getting to the Root

One very important aspect of the exploration of our insensitivity is discovering its root. I have found that there are two basic roots; the first is fear and the second is being conditioned to suppress our vulnerability and to learn to survive at any cost.

In the consciousness of the wounded child, we are fear based. In those moments when our actions lack respectfulness of others, we are being driven by this fear. Until we deal with it, as much as we would like to be respectful and sensitive, all our good intentions are pointless because they do not go to the root. To heal our insensitivity, we have to understand where they are coming from rather than judging them or trying to fix them. I have always felt that in many ways I was selfish and that deep down, saw little outside the narrow context of my own wants and needs. I hid it well, but I felt horribly guilty about it.

I was conditioned to be giving and caring for others and in some ways, I was always rebelling against this programming. As much as I wanted to be sensitive to others, my selfishness was partly a way of saying that I did not want to be "good". I wanted to find myself first.

Morality is no substitute for self-discovery although our culture tries to make it one.

Sensitivity, compassion, caring and awareness of others come from self-awareness. To start a process of learning compassion, we have to shed the skin of our conditioning and find out who we are. Before that we may launch into guilt motivated efforts of trying to be kind, considerate and righteous, but it is hollow. When I first met my master, I was relieved when I heard him challenging all these moralistic approaches to "right" living. What we need, he said, is awareness not morality. Then right action arises by itself. Otherwise, we continue to repress.

Our unawareness and lack of sensitivity to others arise because in the child state of consciousness, we are so focused on our own survival. We can deal with our fears and insecurities either with meditation and allow ourselves to accept and feel the fear or we can move into our survival strategies. Meditation gives the inner panicked child a nourishing and containing presence that relaxes the fear, parenting ourselves with meditative consciousness. In the absence of meditation, our survival strategies take over, which by their very nature are not sensitive to others.

Our lack of sensitivity and respectfulness also comes from a deep conditioning. It is usually patterned on the energy and behavior that we learned from our caretakers in childhood. If one of our parents was tyrannical, we not only became a victim but we also learned to become a tyrant. We often become both the abused and the abuser. It just depends on who we are with. There is a wonderful scene in one of Danny Kaye's movies where a leading officer abuses his immediate inferior who passes it on down the line. When it finally reaches Danny Kaye who is at the end of the pecking order, he has no one to abuse so he kicks a dog that innocently happens to be close by. Most of us do the same thing in our life, simply unconsciously acting out a childhood drama. The process of coming back to ourselves with love and understanding changes this state of affairs. This presence provides more spaciousness inside, more ability to step back from the unconscious behavior. I have seen it work inside me.

2) Inviting Feedback

With more inner space, we also have more ability to explore our unawareness. We are less identified with our strategies and can look at them more objectively. If there is a sincere willingness to uncover and work with the part of us that is disrespectful, un-aware, entitled and selfish, something changes. To do that, we have to watch our reactive-entitled child in action. One way to do that is to invite feedback.

We reach a turning point in our transformation into consciousness when we open our insensitivity and unawareness for feedback from those who are close to us. It is like making an open admission to ourselves as well as to others that we have blind spots and would like help to see through them. We are nurturing a deep desire to lead our life in a less violent way. I have found it very supportive in my life to be with a group of friends who have made this kind of commitment to their growth to giving and receiving feedback from each other.

Openly, or just energetically, we can ask our lovers and friends, *"In what ways do you feel that I am insensitive or not respectful to you, or in what ways do you feel I invade your boundaries?"*

This question creates a structure where one person opens his or herself to loving feedback and the other is given permission to share what normally is difficult to talk about. Practically, in our daily life, we can make a contract with friends and lovers to let each other know in a non-attacking way when we are not being respectful to each other. It builds much trust and intimacy to bring our unawareness and insensitivity out of the closet, expose them for feedback and not be so attached to being a saint. We can get furious with someone who has been disrespectful to us, but often the anger vanishes the minute we feel he or she is sincerely willing to look at how they might have hurt us.

Some of us were very powerful as children, able to manipulate and control our parents and the situation around us to get what we wanted. Since it worked so well, we naturally continue to do it in relationships with our lover and friends today. Somewhere, we may be secretly looking for someone who is strong enough to set limits on us. Our relationships become power struggles. No healing starts to happen until we sincerely create a willingness to see our "stuff" and not wait for someone to call us on it. Our insensitivities are dark corners, stubborn areas of our personality structure that often seem impenetrable. It sometimes seems that our deepest survival mechanisms just don't want to come into the light and be healed. But if our commitment to healing and to opening is deep, these corners melt away.

3) Feeling the Pain of Unawareness

At the deepest level, the most powerful tool for gaining respect for others is simply *feeling the pain of our unawareness*. Some of the most painful moments in my life have been when I recognized the pain I caused by my insensitivity to those I have been close to. One incident stands out in particular. When I was a teenager, I was very involved in playing tennis. My mother was having her first major exhibition of her sculpture and I arrived late at the opening because I was finishing a game. I did not even realize that she had been hurt or even how much it meant to her until, with tears in her eyes, she shared with me the next day that she had wished I had come on time. I went into my room and wept. It struck me how self-centered I was, not only on this occasion, but in many situations in my life.

I suspect that we don't want to feel or see our insensitivity because we are afraid that we will feel so badly about ourselves. When I allow myself to feel that pain, the first place it triggers in me often is much guilt and shame. It is easy to begin judging myself: "How could I be so insensitive?" "I'm such a bad person, so selfish and inconsiderate." "How could anyone love or respect someone who is so uncaring?" These are some of the common voices that pop up in my head. I can also easily go automatically into trying to defend myself.

But it is important to find that space inside where we can accept and expose our insensitivity. If we can accept it, we can heal it. We are all on the road to healing and a big piece of this healing is to accept that we are still unconscious at times. It is only our unconsciousness that creates insensitivity. And it is precisely the pain of seeing how we hurt that heals. It is strong and deep enough to get under our defenses and our obsessions with our own survival and it causes a profound shift in our consciousness.

When we leave bloody tracks in our wake, we don't get the self-love and self-respect that we are looking for so desperately.

I have not found any simple way to learn the lessons of awareness and respect. It comes slowly as part of a general commitment to bring more awareness and light into my life. I certainly have to give myself plenty of space to make mistakes and to be unconscious, remembering that a panicked child is not conscious; he is obsessed with meeting his needs. With deeper understanding and meditation, the fears become less compelling and less dominant.

Respect Comes from Spaciousness

We have been looking, in these two chapters, at the process of gaining back self-respect by honoring our boundaries and our integrity and by learning to become more caring, graceful and considerate. Basically, it is not two different processes; it is one and the same. By becoming more aware of our own boundaries, we become aware of others' boundaries. By feeling the pain of invading another's space, we feel the pain when ours is invaded. In both cases, it is a process of coming back home, of seeing that our fears don't need to run our life, our fears of confronting or exposing ourselves to others, our fears of seeing our own insensitivity. With meditation, we create more space in the belly, more distance, more ability to dis-identify from the panicked child who compromises and who invades. Inner spaciousness brings back respect.

Exercise 1: Sharing Withholds

Pick the most significant people in your life and imagine one at a time that each is sitting in front of you.

- What have you not shared with this person?
- Is there anything that you are withholding from saying?
- What is it that causes you to withhold?
- Is there any way that you feel that this person is insensitive to you?
- As you share, see if anger or protection arises. Notice where that energy comes from in the body
- Is it hard to stay vulnerable with this person? Why?

Exercise 2: Awareness of Respect

Pick a few of the most significant people in your life, including your lover and write down the ways that you feel you are not sensitive or respectful of their space. Notice how you get what you want from them. What strategies do you use?

******

Chapter 19

The Delicate Dance of Melting and Separating

Our ability to be alone is not really tested until we have opened to someone and, even more, stayed open. Before that, aloneness is more isolation than anything else. Intimacy brings us face to face with the terrifying fear of loss and of rejection. It also brings us face to face with our fears that if we open, we will become lost in the other person. Dealing with these two fears – the fear of separation and the fear of engulfment – is one of the basic challenges and rewards of intimacy. Relating intimately is certainly one arena where we can heal these fundamental wounds.

The Fears of Separation

When I explore my own separation fears, I discover that there is a hunger deep inside to know that the person who loves me will never leave. Not even for a short time. I want to feel that I will never be rejected or abandoned. I suspect that many of us have similar fears. The fears show themselves in our relating in all sorts of small and large ways, from something seemingly trivial as how we separate when we are going to be apart, or something as large as when we suspect that our lover is interested in someone or no longer loves us. If we find the courage to open, it brings up an ever-present fear that the other person could leave at any moment.

While in my role as an anti-dependent, I had no idea how I was traumatizing my lovers whenever I reacted with one of my fits of "independence". I was so disconnected from my own fears that I could not see how I was provoking so much separation anxiety in my partners. But hiding behind my anti-dependency, I was also feeling precisely the same fear that they felt. My anti-dependency was covering my own fear that any moment my lover could leave me. I just was not in touch with it. Not until I allowed myself to open could I finally see my fears of rejection and my unworthiness. Our shame, our insecurities and our fears of

229

abandonment and rejection are so strong that the slightest empathic failure from our lovers can provoke and validate our fears. Our fears of separation will seize on the slightest thing to make us feel rejected or abandoned. Separating is terrifying because we have no assurance that the love will return. So we cling.

I have often wondered where so much fear comes from. In my psychiatric training, I learned that the fear of separation apparently comes from being deprived of basic nurturing in some way quite early in life – either in utero or in the first year of life, creating a deep wound of mistrust. It corresponds to what psychologist Erik Erickson has called the first major developmental stage where we learn either basic trust or mistrust. I suspect that most of us have some deep primal traumas from this early time in our lives pushed into the unconscious that causes us to have profound separation anxieties. It was a big surprise for me to uncover these issues and to feel how deeply they had affected my trust. We all have to face the existential fact of our aloneness and with the unpredictability and insecurity of things. But our unhealed traumas of childhood can make the process of accepting and surrendering to so much insecurity very frightening.

Me and Not-Me

Our fears of separation come up in our intimate relating in what I call the "me and not-me" phenomenon. During the early phase of a relationship, we are trapped in a "me" delusion. What I mean is that we somehow believe and feel that we and our lover are the same. (In psychology, this is called "symbiosis".) We see and feel things the same way. We have a similar perspective on important things. It can be re-enforced by sharing common goals, religions, gurus, politics, even taste in movies and so on. But in time, it gets harder and harder to maintain this delusion. Little things show us that the other is not as "me" as we thought. Then comes the painful feeling that we are not as alike in our souls as we thought and unless we can accept the "not me" aspects, the fear can come in that we have made a big mistake. We try to hide this with denial, but eventually it becomes obvious that more and more

230

"not-me" is creeping in.

The "not me" realizations bring up abandonment fears. I think that many couples try to cover up these realizations, because it is painful to face the abandonment and the fears of isolation. When the "not me" realizations arise, we begin to doubt if we can share our deepest self with the other. One way to cover up the "not-me" feelings is just to keep the relationship shallow. Each person gets involved in his and her separate life and never has to face this pain. When they come together, it is more routine rather than deep sharing. Even the sexuality avoids deep connecting. Another obvious way to avoid feeling "not-me" is to focus on trying to change the other person. I worked hard at it. I did whatever I could to get my partners more into meditation, more into moving their bodies, more into doing seminars with me, into whatever I was into. And my lovers tried to make me more receptive, more feminine and more available. It didn't work. What it brought instead was continual conflict, misunderstanding and pain.

Then what do we do? Usually, we create some kind of a drama to end the relationship and by changing partners, we can maintain the delusion that someday, with the right person, we will find someone where there are no "not-me" feelings. It can't happen. The experience of "not-me" is inevitable. It brings up the separation wound and we have to face it. Eventually we recognize that in some deep and significant ways, we are different and we can't always communicate or connect that it is not the difference that brings the painful feelings of separation. Sooner or later, it will present itself in any deep relationship and we have to face it, not just with lovers, but with friends as well.

Accepting the "not me" is an important maturing process. It brings us face to face with our aloneness. Relationships often bring us our first rude encounters with aloneness. The deeper we go with someone, the more painful the "not-me" feelings can be because it is juxtaposed against the moments of deep melting. We have to deal with our expectations that we will find someone who is all "me". We have to wake up from the dream. Dealing with our separation fears means slowly facing the "not-me" feelings.

231

Realizing the insecurity, acknowledging the differences and still keeping the heart open is quite a meditation.

The intensity of our fears of separation really does not arise until we make a sincere commitment to sustain intimacy with someone.

As long as we remain anti-dependent and as long as we keep a back door open in our love affairs, we don't enter into the room of fear. But by hanging in and committing, we enter this frightening room and confront our fears. The important point is not that we guarantee to the other that we will never leave. That is not possible. But we stop avoiding our fears of separation with games. We are always facing the possibility of loss and eventually we will have to face it one way or another. The challenge of love is to keep opening anyway.

I have found it healing for me to recognize and accept how deep these fears are and how easily they can be provoked when I become vulnerable. Before, I judged these feelings both in myself and in others and I developed a spiritual ego that repressed them. Since I have begun to accept and work with the fear, I recognize them in others almost universally. I have come to see that opening to them is a very important part of my spiritual journey, part of my softening and my opening.

The Fears of Melting and of Intimacy

A few days ago, I ran into a friend who was separating from her boyfriend of five years. He was having an affair with a teenager and had become involved with drugs. She was beating herself up because she felt that he left her because she was too old and too serious. Truth is, he was terrified of intimacy and was just acting out. He had not wanted to deal with his fears. In fact, he was not even aware that he had them. For him, relationship was still about being "in his energy". When problems arise, it's time to move on. It amazes me that we can stay in a relationship so long and still not have faced our deeper wounds of melting and separating. I know because I did. And I even thought that I was in a deep intimate connection!

Our fears of intimacy can be very deep and unconscious. We create all kinds of ways to avoid facing them. Our previous experiences may have made us phobic of letting another person come close. When we do, we react and create separation; dramatically, mindlessly and often vengefully. Rather than look at our patterns, we get lost in them. Once we create a little or a lot of separation, we want closeness again; pulling in, pushing away, needy child and rebellious child going back and forth. But in this process, we never look at what is deeper. We may never actually face the fear.

When I became aware of my anti-dependency, I saw that my need for "space" (which is one of the most sacred words of anti-dependents) was not real. By saying that I needed my "space", I was not looking deeply enough inside. What did I mean by "space"? What was it space that I really wanted? What I discovered was that at the bottom, I was looking to find myself, not "space". I was not going to come any closer to finding myself by taking "space" and just being alone. That aloneness needed to be part of a sincere commitment to find myself. Because of our shame, it is hard to validate our need for time to find ourselves. We always have to give ourselves away for love and are so afraid that if we do take time to go in, we will be punished for it.

I took space, but I felt guilty much of the time. Why? Because I wanted permission to find myself. I wasn't validating my need to find myself or taking the risk of meeting disapproval when I did. The guilt created anger and reaction because it is coming out of my unclarity. Naturally, I was projecting on my lovers that they were the ones who were preventing me from being free, from finding myself or from being alone. When we are trapped in any kind of projection, we become convinced that the other is responsible and it leaves little room for us to see what is really happening inside.

There is a second reason, that our compulsive need for "space" is not real. It is often a way of running from confronting our fears of coming close. I could not see my terror because I was not dealing with it. Among men, these feelings – the fear of being controlled, the guilt for wanting to be alone, the reactiveness toward women and the false self-reliance are very common. Our relationships with women become an unconscious acting out of anger and fears of opening again to the mothering energy. The paradox is that while we move away out of fear of domination, it does nothing to bring us back into our power. We cannot become empowered until we confront the fears.

For women, I think the process of melting, though much more invited and familiar also brings up fears of being dominated. Many women have been deeply conditioned to be dependent and subservient to men. When they begin to recover from this programming, there often arises a strong reaction to the paternalistic and patronizing energy of their fathers and of the male oriented culture in general that has belittled and infantilized women. To open to a man brings back the fear of losing identity and power and becoming subservient once again.

In coming out of isolation and risking to stay open, I have also had to deal with feelings of shame of not knowing how to relate intimately and the fear that I just don't have the skills to share and to be there emotionally for someone. When I came out of my denial and saw my fears, I could see that the only reason I judged intimate sharing was because I didn't understand what it was or how to do it. I was never given the tools. I was not accustomed to exposing and sharing my intimate feelings. I was not even aware that I had them. I was conditioned to be a "doer" and I was always very good at it. I learned to enjoy doing things, but I have had a much harder time learning to "be". Intimate sharing is much more about sharing our "being" than it is about sharing our "doing". For someone not raised in an environment where deep intimate communication was the rule (which I suspect is the case for most of us), he or she must learn a whole new way to be with people to open and sustain intimacy.

The process of learning to melt, to confront our fears of losing ourselves in the other is a big challenge. I noticed that opening put me into shock much of the time and I found myself slipping back to my old patterns of hiding in my isolation. When the shock set in, I pulled back and cut off in spite of my desire to confront the fears. I couldn't tell what I wanted anymore. I couldn't tell whether I wanted to be alone or to be with the other. I was too shocked to feel anything. I couldn't even communicate what was happening in me. But being with this shock with all its numbness and confusion is a big part of the process of opening again.

At a certain point, it became clear to me that if I wanted love, I had to be willing to confront my shame and my fears of closeness. Practically, that meant making a conscious decision to stay connected and to feel and share what comes up all the time, to continue relating openly and honestly even when every cell in my body wanted to run away. I finally saw that I could never actually see what I was afraid of until I confronted it consciously. Even making a conscious choice to confront these fears doesn't make it easy. I recognize my pattern to run all the time. It is right in front of me. I also have to face my fears and guilt about taking time to be alone. But when I share these with my lover, I am able to see that we both have similar fears. Fundamentally, we are facing the same challenges.

Learning How to Melt

When I first explored this dance between melting and separating, I thought that it conveniently followed the lines of the dependent and the anti-dependent. The dependent covered up his or her fears of separating with dependency and the anti-dependent covered his or her fears of intimacy with isolation. But now I see that the dichotomy is false. All of us have deep fears of both separation and of melting. These two styles are only superficial protections of our fears. Once we begin to earnestly explore the fears, our identification with the roles disappears.

The drama between the dependent and the anti-dependent is only the first level of our journey. Without awareness and commitment, we remain at this lower level.

But the dance of learning to melt and separate is at a much higher level. At this point, we recognize that both of us have deep wounds of melting and separating to deal with and we come together to work on them together.

With that kind of understanding, compassion and commitment, the story can become very different. We come together already aware that both of us have a deeply wounded heart and we have to tread lightly and sensitively. Smallest things will trigger either wound.

There are some basic reasons that make the dance difficult. First, our timings can be different. One person wants to dance toward separation while another wants to dance toward melting. When that happens, the child inside can freak out. Up come our abandonment wounds, our fears of not being understood, respected, supported and loved. The one who wants separation feels squeezed and controlled and the one who wants melting feels abandoned. Unless we process this when it arises, we have pain and conflict. In an atmosphere of spaciousness, respect and willingness to listen and understand the other person, we can work with this timing problem when it comes up.

Another difficulty is that one or both are not willing or don't give themselves permission to be total in the melting or the separating. That creates a confused, murky energy. I recognize this vividly in myself. I still have guilt feelings when I want to take time to be alone. That sends out a vibration to my lover that is confusing because she can feel that I am not giving myself the space I need and she begins to wonder what I want. She can sense my hesitation and my lack of totality. Also, when I don't validate that alone space and give it to myself, I get resentful and am not present when we are together, only creating more murkiness. The dance does not flow if we are not committed to both aspects of it; finding the courage to be alone when we need it and the courage to share deeply when we are together.

Learning How to Separate

Another area that needs love and sensitivity is the way in which we separate. It is painful to cut off abruptly or inexplicably. To the child, this is violent. We all need our space, our time to be alone, to be creative, to recharge and to find ourselves again. When this need arises, we have to take it, *but how we take it makes all the difference.* If we can stay sensitive to the other person when we pull away or take space, it may actually not rekindle the wound of being abandoned (or at least not nearly so much). When our lover separates graciously and communication is open, our panic is not so likely to come up because, by communicating, we remain connected.

Furthermore, it is not our lover's job to give us permission to leave and take time for ourselves. If we want this guarantee, we will never grow up. It helps in dancing this dance to stay aware that we will be triggering the other person's separation wound when we take time for ourselves and also our own and we have to face it. As long as we do everything "right", we never have to face our own fears that the other person could take revenge, cut off, get angry or whatever. These possibilities bring up our own fears of being alone. Our separation wound will be triggered. There is no imaginable way, nor is it right for our growth that we are shielded from feeling these fears. We have to invite it. If we cling to the romantic notion that the other will be there for us at all times, or that we have to be there for him or her at all times, we have sabotaged ourselves from the beginning.

It helps to share with our lover or friend our fears of taking time and space for ourselves. Let them know our story. Then, at least, there is some understanding to build a foundation of trust. It is also good to share our wound of being abandoned when the other person takes space and time. Once we know each others wounds and fears, it will be much easier for him or her to become sensitive to how he or she triggers it. Sharing our past with each other is one of the ways we get close. This is true for close friends, not just our lover. Not that it necessarily makes it any easier when the hurt actually happens, but it does help to bring us back to the heart.

What makes this dance so challenging is that our wounds are deep and easily triggered. Furthermore, from our childhood, we are accustomed to being betrayed. A couple I saw recently illustrated this clearly. He had made love to another woman who happened to be his lover's best friend and not just once, but over many months. She is a recovering incest victim and has deep fears and insecurities about her sexuality. He had this affair years ago but he had withheld telling her because he was afraid of her reaction. Now they are trying to build back the trust. She is torn between feelings of love and forgiveness on the one hand and on the other, rage and wanting revenge. He feels alternately guilty and impatient.

The dance involves sharing all the time, even with what seem to be the most trivial incidents that trigger our hurts. In our ongoing relationships in the smallest ways, we push each other's abandonment/deprivation wounds all the time. And then it's easy to invalidate ourselves and each other when they come up. "Oh, don't be silly. You don't have to feel that way", or "I can't understand why you should feel that way. You're making much too much out of this." If the hurt is there, it's there and it is another opportunity to share and get closer to each other. It doesn't matter if the trigger seems trivial or not. The feelings are not trivial.

Love and Meditation

The dance of separating and melting runs a full spectrum of consciousness.

At the lowest level, at the level of the drama of the anti-dependent and dependent, we are still trapped in misunderstanding and projection. At a higher level, our journey together becomes two friends on the path of truth, teaching each other from our own strengths and experiences about aloneness and melting and sharing the pain and fears involved in each. On the highest level, we have integrated the parts that we have disowned and rejected

238

and can relate equally to both processes as they arise.

Exercise: Exploring Melting and Separation

1) Melting

Take a moment to reflect and perhaps write down the fears that you have regarding allowing someone to come close. Imagine that your lover is sitting opposite to you and presenting you with the opportunity to come closer.

This exploration is most poignant with a lover but it comes up with anyone we allow ourselves any closeness with. See what comes up in responding to the following statements:

- If I let you in you will ...

- If I show you who I am you will ...

2) Separating

Exploring the other polarity, what are our fears of separating and letting go? If we look closely, it may be that we see it differently than we thought. We will explore it two ways – how it feels to be the one who separates and how it feels to be the one who is separated from. Separating takes many forms. Sometimes when we separate, we feel in synchronicity with each other, both desiring space. Other times, one of us wants it, the other doesn't. And these two experiences feel quite different.

As you answer these questions, again imagine that you are seated opposite your lover but recognizing also that it could apply to anyone in your life.

- Can you tell when you would like to separate and take space for yourself?

- When you want to take space for yourself, do you follow this energy or do you bind yourself in responsibility and guilt?

- What do you search for when you take some emotional and physical distance?

- Do you find that even when you are with someone you always keep distance, or are there times when you really allow melting?

- When you separate, do you say anything or just go?

- What arises for you when your lover pulls his or her energy away from you without saying anything?

- Is it different when you feel his or her leaving physically, but still connected emotionally?

******

Chapter 20

Letting Go - into Love and Aloneness

"You are always on the move. The reality is here and you are always on the move, hence there happens no meeting. Unless that meeting happens, you will never be happy. Happiness is when you are in tune with reality. Happiness is a harmony between you and the real. Unhappiness in a disharmony between you and the real. So if you are unhappy, remember, you must be going away from reality.

You have to follow reality; you have to come in a deep accordance with reality, in tune with it. You have to become a note in the great orchestra that reality is. Not fighting but surrendering, submitting to it, ready to dissolve into it. That is love – the readiness to dissolve into reality; the readiness to merge, melt; the readiness to be one with reality. You will be losing something – your dreams, your ego; you will be losing that separation. You will disappear as a drop of water, but there is nothing to be worried about, you will become the ocean.

You will not be what you have been up to now – your ego. Your fences will disappear. You will not be an island, but a part of the continent. Nothing is lost by losing yourself, everything is lost by resisting."

Osho · The Beloved

At the end of our journey out of fear, embracing a life of love and meditation, we come to the greatest challenge of all – letting go. I recognize that all my little fights, my efforts to control and manipulate situations and others are just my fight with existence. These are the ways that I hold on and they show me how much more work I have to do inside. We hold on because of our unresolved fear.

To begin to let go of our control strategies, we have to trust – to trust that existence will provide us with what we need. For me,

241

this is my constant meditation. It means opening to insecurity, to the fear of not getting what I want and all the fears that follow that. If I let go of trying to control or manipulate the outside, I have to accept my fears and feel them. I am making a conscious choice to go into them. Any frustration, disappointment, discomfort or threat produces an instant reaction of trying to control, manipulate or in some way change the outside so the threat disappears. And each time we are covering up fear or pain. These small situations arise in all of our lives all the time. They are not trivial. Letting go means turning the focus in. Instead of controlling the outside, we feel what is triggered inside.

Our strategies take us away from ourselves. I have discovered that when I do make the choice to go in, the fear and the pain are not ever what I anticipated that they would be. In fact, the pain and fear come when I lose myself, not when I don't get what I want from the outside. It arises out of losing my center. Slowly, I am seeing that my nourishment comes not from getting my wants and needs met from the outside, but from going in, from returning over and over again to myself, from the sheer joy of self-discovery and from recovering my center.

Still, I am constantly having to remind myself to let go of my strategies and my focus on the outer and to come back to myself. My conditioning is so strong, and it never supported finding nourishment from going in. Few of us were supported to go in because we were not raised in an atmosphere of meditation. The compulsion to go out is compelling because it is automatic. We have to relearn, to become accustomed to taking those moments of discomfort and going inside with them.

In this last chapter, I go over what I have found to be the key ingredients that support our journey toward letting go and going in.

Moving from "Jockey" to "Saddle" Position

In our workshops, we use a simple metaphor to support learning to let go and go in. When a threat or disappointment comes, we react. Reaction is our survival, our instinctual response to threat. We call this reactive stance, "the jockey position", because our energy is up and directed forward toward the goal of altering the outside. In contrast, when we are settled back with ourselves, giving ourselves space to feel, watch and allow, we call, "sitting back in the saddle". In this position, we are seated in ourselves, in our inner chair in a sense and we consciously turn off the instinctual impulse to react. Sitting in the saddle is a letting go and a going in. When we give ourselves that kind of space, our intelligence and intuition has time to operate. We give space for the inner knower to respond to the trigger in whatever way feels appropriate.

I watch this mechanism closely in my relating. At those moments where I feel misunderstood or suspect that I am being manipulated or attacked, or when I feel abandoned, it is so compelling to launch into blame and fight or retreat into my familiar resignation. I can actually feel the pull to defend, to push away or to take revenge. Without awareness at those moments, I would move automatically into the "jockey position", pulled by an ancient compulsion of survival. I can feel the energy centered in my solar plexus – the energy of fight, defend, strike out or give up. My child inside is saying, "See, there it goes again. No one understands me. I am totally alone and if I don't protect myself, I am going to be taken advantage of." It is an energy of hurt, anger and resignation – an old movie based on childhood traumas that I have run and rerun many times.

There is no value for my growth to remain in the movie of my conditioning. This is a moment when I can take a risk and try something new. That risk is to consciously stop the reaction from my solar plexus and drop the energy into my belly. That means letting go of wanting to change the outside and to go in and feel. From the saddle, in my belly, I have more space to recognize that my deprivation and abandonment wound is being provoked and stay with the feelings.

To the other person, instead of reacting, I say something like, "I am feeling like we are getting caught in fight. I don't want to go into fight. Actually, I am feeling hurt about what you said because ..." Or, "I feel as if I have to protect myself right now because I am afraid that ...". In those moments, we are actually taking the energy out of the solar plexus and bringing it down into the belly. From that place, the other person no longer feels attacked. By making that move, we are taking the responsibility to stop the fight. It always takes two to fight. If one of us stops, moves down into the belly and is willing to be vulnerable, the fight stops.

When we choose not to react, we invite vulnerability. In fact, our reaction is precisely so we don't have to feel helpless and vulnerable. In relationships, whether it is with lovers or friends, we always want the other person to be the first to be vulnerable. We like to stay safe and protected, waiting for the other to make the first step. It hurts our pride to be vulnerable first. We would rather be right and on top, to prove to the other person that he or she should feel sorry and look at his blind spots. It is deeply frightening to let go of this need to be right and in control. Yet, we can't have love or meditation as long as we are holding onto our desire to be right, in control or safe.

Tracing Back from the Trigger to the Wound

There is another understanding that helps with the process of moving from fight to vulnerability, from control to letting go and going in. When our wound gets triggered, we can trace a sequence of events that happen inside, from trigger to reaction. Under the reaction is our hurt or fear. The trigger activates an expectation and the expectation is covering a wound of early deprivation. Instead of feeling or sharing the hurt, we react by judging, blaming or cutting off.

A small example: I wrote a friend of mine an email recently sharing some intimate and painful circumstances that were happening in my life at the time. For one reason or another, he didn't respond for a few weeks. During that time, I felt myself cutting off and pulling away from him. Inside, I started also to judge him for not being sensitive and for not living up to my idea of a friend. His not responding was the trigger. My expectation was that when I open my heart, I should get a response soon. When the expectation was not met, I reacted. The reaction was covering up an early wound of not being listened to and now I expect that no one will be there to listen. But how often do we make the commitment to trace back to the wound and share it? We react instead, which only causes more pain and misunderstanding. As I have said previously, our expectations and our reactions are only a result of our deprivation.

That wounded little kid inside expects, because he or she feels so starved for love. If we can identify the expectation and trace back to the wound of deprivation that it is covering, we are back in the saddle. We don't have to get rid of the expectation, we don't have to get rid of anything, we only need to bring awareness to what is going on inside. No matter what the trigger, whether it is friend, lover or environment, the same sequence is set into motion. Following the sequence back from trigger to expectation to deprivation wound is an awareness tool that we can practice and share with our lover and close friends all the time.

Embracing Our Fears on the Path to Surrender

Letting go takes us to our vulnerability and when we are vulner-able, we encounter our fears. It is helpful to know that these fears belong to a young and regressed part of us that still carries body memories of trauma. Feeling this fear is the first stop on the path of surrender to existence. When we relinquish our survival strategies, up comes fear, because all these survival strategies resulted from fear and lack of trust in the first place. *Therefore, letting go has no value unless we embrace our fears as part of our search for truth.*

Before I was more intimate with my fears, I pushed them aside because I considered them regressed, childish and self indulgent. The letting go that I did came more from a resignation than a

245

genuine surrender. When I felt helpless, I pretended that I didn't care. But that didn't get me any closer to feeling what was really happening inside. A genuine letting go is when we care tremendously, but still we let go of trying to change the outer. Looking back, I can see that I coped with most of my major rejections in the past by minimizing how deeply it hurt and frightened me. When we don't embrace our fears, we split off our vulnerability and it becomes disowned. From this disowned place, it continues to exert a powerful influence, but it does it surreptitiously. We create an inner split between the "the wild one" - the adventurer-explorer inside and our vulnerable side - the one who carries our fears, insecurities, receptivity and softness.

A client I saw recently illustrated the polarity that occurs when we disown our fears. She was apprehensive because she was about to leave India and return to Germany to be with her boyfriend, but was doubting if she still wanted to be with him. "He is boring," she told me. "I don't feel sexually turned onto him anymore. He doesn't want to take risks and do new things, he doesn't meditate and he doesn't want to work on himself."

I asked her to imagine that there were two sides to her. On her left was her vulnerable side and on her right was her wild side. From the right side, she continued to complain about how uninteresting her boyfriend was and how little she was attracted to him sexually. But when I asked her to move over to the other side, everything changed. She immediately started to cry and expressed how much she needed him, how safe and cared for she felt with him and how the thought of being without him was simply terrifying. Exploring further, she could see that inside her, there was also a split between her seeker and her vulnerability. Neither one was particularly trusting or sensitive of the other. Her relationship was reflecting this split.

Finally, when I asked her to sit between these two positions, she could appreciate the split much more easily. It was clearly not time for her to make any decision about being with her boyfriend or not. But it was important for her to begin integrating these two parts of her, becoming more sensitive to the needs and characteristics of each. With such a radical split inside, she would not find someone who could meet both the needs of her wounded child who needed much safety and security and her seeker who craved adventure and the unknown.

Embracing our frightened side is a crucial piece of our work on ourselves that requires much care, patience and trust. It is so easy to escape into our reactive-entitled child – that practiced politician and strategist. Many situations, particularly our intimate relationships, can mirror for us just how much of a split we have created inside between the part of us that copes with and avoids fears and the one who carries them.

Playing the Edge

We can envision our life and each aspect of it, even the most trivial situations, as an opportunity to play our fear edge. *Every situation we face and create in life gives us the opportunity to play our fear edge.* When we don't embrace these challenges, we fight them. We become victims, blaming others or outside events for bringing us discomfort or disappointment.

A couple I saw recently was having trouble because she felt he was unreachable and he felt she was too demanding. Very common situation. When we explored more deeply, we discovered that he, although very self-confident and an ardent seeker, was terrified of his vulnerability. When I framed for him that going into his sensitive side was the very place where he needed to grow and build courage, he could embrace it because it satisfied his seeker side. Similarly for her, being less demanding when she felt frustrated brought her up against her fears of being deprived and this seemed to be her fear edge – the place where she could grow.

******

Conclusion

Our conditioning does not give us much support to let go and trust. It deludes us into believing in the hope that someone or something will take our pain and fear away. It does not support the inner road that can lead to genuine recovery. It does not support meditation. If we want to find ourselves again and rebuild our trust in life, there is no alternative but to uncover our denial and delusions and to go in and face the fears and pain. That is the path of introspection and meditation, embracing what life brings us as food for growth; just watching, feeling and allowing.

Letting go into trust also involves a deep acceptance of our aloneness, not an aloneness that arises out of isolation and fear of closeness, but from a simple recognition of the "isness" of it. I cannot honestly say that I have arrived at the point of totally accepting my aloneness or my death. But I have reached the point of no longer trying to control things so compulsively and unconsciously. Letting go is the only way that we can bring love into our lives. Before that, we are simply pushing love away the very people whom we go to for nourishment and closeness with all of our control strategies. Letting go is a process of surrendering to the unknown and to the mystery, not just random acts of surrender, but allowing it to become a lifestyle of coming closer and closer to trust.

I end by sharing a story my master once told us. It is a story of a Chinese emperor who was a great lover of art and painting. He invited all the painters of his kingdom to come together for a great competition to determine who was the master painter. He promised as a reward many riches and a part of his kingdom. Thousands of painters gathered from all over the land. But one old painter approached the emperor and said that he would participate in the competition only with certain conditions. First of all, it would take him three years to complete the painting. Secondly, no one was to be allowed to see the painting until it was completed.

249

The king agreed reluctantly recognizing that this old man had a quality that was unique and appealing. All the other painters completed their works within a month. None satisfied the emperor. Meanwhile, he waited for the old man to complete his painting. He had given him a large room in the palace surrounded by many guards to ensure that no one would enter before it was done. The emperor waited three years. When the work was completed, the painter invited the emperor to come and view it. It covered an entire wall of the palace and the scene it depicted was a landscape. In the front was a beautiful forest and behind, towering mountains. In the middle of the painting was a path leading through the forest toward the mountains and it gradually wound its way out of sight up into the mountains.

The emperor could not believe his eyes. Never had he seen something so beautiful, so miraculous, so magical. After a long silence, he asked the painter only one question. "I am very much interested in this little footpath that goes around the forest; it is seen sometimes around the mountains and then disappears. Where does it go?"

The painter said, "There is no way to know unless you walk on it."

The emperor, overwhelmed by the beauty and grandeur of the work of art, totally forgot that it was just a painting. He took the artist by the hand and they both walked along the path and disappeared into the mountains. They have not yet returned.

We are each taking a long, sometimes blissful, sometimes intensely painful journey through the forest and gradually are making our way up the mountain. Our co-dependency struggles are, in a way, the dark forest. But the end point of our journey takes us high into the mountains beyond the realm of the known and the familiar. Our quest is to find ourselves and in the process to share a deep love with another person. The painter takes us each by the hand and gently guides us onto a path whose destination is unknown and unknowable.

"Be a child again and you will not be running away from your-self. You will be running within yourself – and that is the way of the meditator. The worldly man runs away from himself and the seeker runs within himself to find the source of this life, this consciousness. And when he discovers the source, he has discovered not only his life source, he has discovered the life source of the universe, the whole cosmos. A tremendous celebration arises in him. Life becomes just a song, a dance, moment to moment."

Osho · Satyam, Shivam, Sunderam

Selected References

Almaas, A-Hameed Ali: The Pear Beyond Price; Diamond Publications, Berkeley, CA 1900

Almass, A-Hameed Ali: The Diamond Heart Series Books 1,2 and 3. Diamond Publications, Berkeley, CA 1986

Bradshaw, John: The Family; Health Communications, Inc,. Deerfield Beach, FL 1988

Bradshaw, John: Homecoming, Health Communications, Inc., Deerfield FL 1990

Bradshaw, John: Creating Love Bantam Books, NY, NY 1992

Bradshaw, John: Healing the Shame that Binds You, Bantam Books, NY, NY 1988

Carter, Forest: The Education of Little Tree, University of New Mexico Press, Albuquerque, NM 1976

Horney, Karen: Neurosis and Human Growth, W.W. Norton, NY, NY 1950

Horney, Karen: The Neurotic Person of Our Time, W.W. Norton, NY, NY 1950

Kaufman, Gershan: Shame, The Power of Caring, Schinkman Books, Rochester, Vermont 1992

Mellody, Pia: Facing Co-Dependency; Harper, San Francisco, 1989

Mellody, Pia: Facing Love Addiction; Harper, San Francisco, 1992

Mellody, Pia: The Intimacy Factor, Harper San Francisco, 2003

Mellody, Pia: Breaking Free, A Recovery Workbook for Facing Co-Dependency, Harper, San Fransisco 1989

Miller, Alice: The Drama of the Gifted Child, Basic Books, NY, NY 1980

Miller, Alice: Thou Shalt Not Be Aware, Meridian Penguin Books, NY< NY 1984

Osho: The Path of the Mystic, Rebel Publications, Cologne, Germany and Childvilas Foundation, Scottsdale, AZ 1989

Osho: Beyond Psychology, Rebel Publications, Cologne, Germany and Chidvilas Foundation, Scottsdale, AZ 1990

Osho: Satyam, Shivam, Sunderam; Rebel Publications, Cologne, Germany and Chidvilas Foundation, Scottsdale, AZ 1990

Rinpoche, Sogyal: The Tibetan Book of Living and Dying, Harper San Francisco 1992

Stanford, John: The Invisible Partners – How the Male and the Female in Each of Us Affects Our Relationships, Paulist Press, 1980

Stone, Hal and Winkelman, Sidra: Embracing Ourselves, Nataraj Publications, Novato, CA, 1989

Stone, Hal and Winkelman, Sidra: Embracing Each Other, Nataraj Publications, Novato, CA 1990

CPSIA information can be obtained
at www.ICGtesting.com
Printed in the USA
BVHW061442011218
534527BV00001B/91/P

9 781905 399406